Social Intelligence Skills

Basic Course

DRAFT

Stephen J. Sampson, Ph.D.
Cindy Elrod, Ph.D.

DRAFT

HRD Press, Inc. • Amherst • Massachusetts

Published by: HRD Press, Inc.
                 22 Amherst Road
                 Amherst, MA 01002
                 800-822-2801 (U.S. and Canada)
                 413-253-3488
                 413-253-3490 (fax)
                 www.hrdpress.com

ISBN 978-1-59996-184-2

Production services by Jean Miller
Cover design by Eileen Klockars
Editorial work by Sally M. Farnham

Table of Contents

Module 1: Introduction

Introduction

The Science Behind the Training

Research and experience in the area of interpersonal relationship management have revealed that *successful* interactions among human beings are usually the direct result of the timely and appropriate application of specific and learned interpersonal skills. And it should be no surprise that those same skills are equally effective whether applied at work, at home, or in your community.

Just as our biology and physiology have developed over time, so too have our social skills. And we know that living and working together well takes time, effort, experience, and education. The process is neither automatic nor guaranteed—nor is it ever really finished. Each of our interpersonal interactions influences subsequent interactions. That's why it is so important that we strive, through education and experience, to continually further our social development.

The SoTelligence training program capitalizes on more than four decades of observations and research regarding human interaction. Beginning in the 1960s, the eminent social psychologist Dr. Robert Carkhuff began gathering empirical evidence by studying and observing the interpersonal skills of highly functional individuals and demonstrated that they could be effectively taught by a systematic approach when other necessary conditions of learning were controlled. Building on the tenets of Carl Rogers's "necessary and sufficient conditions of. . . change" (i.e., empathy, congruence, and unconditional positive regard), Carkhuff sought a way to operationalize these dimensions so that they could be researched and taught as skills (Carkhuff, 2000).

Although Carkhuff's model was originally designed with the counseling relationship in mind, it quickly evolved and became an effectively utilized training paradigm across all sorts of contexts. Referred to as Interpersonal Skills Training, Human Technology, and various other metamorphic titles, the essence of the program and the mantra of its founder and trainers is "training as treatment." In other words, utilize clear-cut training in specific skill sets to enhance the abilities of the trainee to attend to his or her own physical, social, emotional, and mental health. With these "states" in order, most individuals will be able to function at higher levels, managing their own behaviors and growth that will lead to successful management of the behaviors and growth of those around them. These positive social *inter*actions are what our daily lives are filled with.

In the classroom, Brigman (1991) found that kindergarten children and teachers who received Carkhuff's interpersonal skills training in attending, listening, and responding skills using a Tell-Show-Do-Feed-back format for instruction demonstrated increases in "school success" behaviors (such as reduced hyperactivity and oppositional behaviors and increased attention, cooperation, and social skills behaviors) along with significant increases in listening and reading comprehension. Further, the children were able to transfer, or generalize, this learning to other areas of achievement. Similar improvements in student performance and cognitive development have been found in other classroom studies of differing age groups and group sizes (Aspy, 1972; Aspy & Roebuck, 1996). Similar findings have been found cross-culturally in academic settings (Aspy & Roebuck, 1996; Rocha, 1985).

In hospitals, physicians who receive and utilize this training during medical consultations receive significantly more and better information from the patient (Aspy et al., 1998).

In a mental health hospital setting, Smoot and Gonzalez (1995) found that when staff were trained, their unit experienced less staff turnover, less sick leave used, less annual leave used, fewer patient complaints, and fewer assaults on staff by patients. This resulted in substantial cost savings for the trained unit.

Twenty-five years after the training was conducted in a community center with "indigenous adult members of the surrounding inner-city" of Springfield, Massachusetts, members who completed the program had exceeded their own expectations. Most had predicted they would live at or near poverty. Instead, *all of them* were in professional or semi-professional positions, many with advanced degrees (personal communication from R. Carkhuff as cited in Aspy et al., 2000).

This training has been found to have profound effects in corrections and juvenile detainment areas. Carkhuff's 1974 book, *Cry Twice!*, follows the implementation of the training in an institution for delinquent boys resulting in 50% increases in physical functioning, 100% increases in emotional functioning, and 15% increases in intellectual functioning while "elopement" status (escape attempts) were reduced by 56%, recidivism rates decreased by 34%, and crime in the area surrounding the institution decreased by 34%. Even more remarkable, the training was given to correctional personnel who had no credentials in mental health, and these correctional personnel delivered the training to the inmates. Another study of learning challenged, delinquent youth resulted in recidivism rates that were 71 to 80% less compared to similar groups that did not receive the training (Collingswood et al., 1978).

Day, et al. (1977), found similar results in a federal corrections setting. Less than one year post-training, the institute reported a savings of over $59,000 (1977 dollars) due to fewer idle days (inmates not reporting for work) and lost accidents (e.g., sabotage). The staff who received the training experienced significantly higher levels of empathy, respect, and genuineness toward the inmates. Additionally, they showed greater tolerance and less authoritarian attitudes toward the inmates. Inmates became more positive in their attitudes and had greater ego strength. They also demonstrated an increase in concern over social responsibility and a decrease in anxiety.

Broward County Sheriff's Office has demonstrated similar findings. Avid promoters of training, they found significantly reduced grievances against staff, assaults against staff, inmate suicide attempts, and use of force by staff on inmates (Ludwig & Barkhurst, 2003; McPherson, 2008).

Ripley (1998) demonstrated the effectiveness of this training on family members with mental illness. In her study of caregivers for patient-relatives, the majority of whom suffered from schizophrenia, she found that caregivers receiving 40 hours of training improved in their knowledge of the brain and brain disorders, understood and were able to perform interpersonal management skills at a competent level, experienced greater cohesion within the family unit, demonstrated more empathy toward the patient's losses while communicating love and support, and experienced greatly reduced stress.

The application of this training to organizational settings has been the subject of many articles and books, including *Interpersonal Skills and Human Productivity* (Carkhuff, 1983a) and *Sources of Human Productivity* (1983b).

These skills have been successfully applied to the training of values (Aspy et al., 1998, 1998a, 1998b, 1998c), multiculturalism (Aspy et al., 1998a; Patterson, 1996), and gender equity (Aspy & Sandhu, 1999).

This short review does not completely capture all of the research, studies, and works/outcomes of the model that began with one man nearly half a century ago, but it does give the reader an idea as to the scope and applicability of this training to virtually any setting, with anyone, at anytime. And speaking of virtually, we have yet to see the impact of this training in a virtual (i.e., web-based) environment, but stay tuned as that is planned in the near future!

The Social Intelligence Skills Model

During this training, you will be exposed to a learning method known as the **Tell-Show-Do-Feedback** model. Each learning module begins with a brief lecture, reading, and written exercises. The skills, sub-skills and sequential steps of the program are shown in Figure 1.

> During this training session, you will be exposed to a learning method known as the **Tell-Show-Do-Feedback** model.

Upon completion of the lecture and exercise, one or more specific skills will be demonstrated to you in a useful context. You will then be given the opportunity to replicate the new skill(s) during role-playing exercises. The instructor and other class participants will give you constructive feedback on your performance. This method of providing interpersonal skills training has been found to be very effective.

Remember, this is a course designed to teach you *skills*. This is not unlike other skills you may have learned such as sports, language, math, computers, etc. According to Dreyfuss (1980), there are five stages to acquiring a skill. First, the learner is a novice. At this point, the learner knows only the most basic and rudimentary components, or rules, around the subject matter. During this state, the instruction process begins by breaking down the skills into their smallest features (or sub-skills) that the learner can recognize. Then, the learner is given rules for determining when and how to apply the subskill. Self-monitoring along with instructional feedback are basic components at this stage as the learner needs them to ensure she or he is "doing it right."

During the competence stage, the student has practiced the subskill and received instructional feedback to the point that the learner begins to see patterns in how to use the subskills and how they "connect" together. This still involves applying the rules and receiving feedback or performing self-monitoring.

The proficiency stage, or third stage, involves even more practice of the subskills and skills in a broader variety of circumstances and contexts. We will experience this in our role plays. This will introduce the learner to applying the rules in novel situations that will broaden the ability to apply the skill correctly.

During the expertise stage, the learner begins to use intuitive responses when applying the skills in novel situations. Until now, the learner has had to rely on step-wise improvement and rules. Now, the "repertoire of experience" is so large due to the amount of practice, feedback, and self-monitoring, the learner is able to associate a specific response to each circumstance or situation.

The final stage of mastery is reached when the learner is capable of experiencing and applying the skills without conscious thought about the appropriate response. It is now a part of the learner's normal performance, and the mental energy previously used to rehearse and think through the application of the skills can be spent on something else.

All of this can sound a little intimidating. Be assured that during and after each session, your questions and thoughts about the training and its applications will be thoroughly addressed.

Figure 1. The Skill Sets

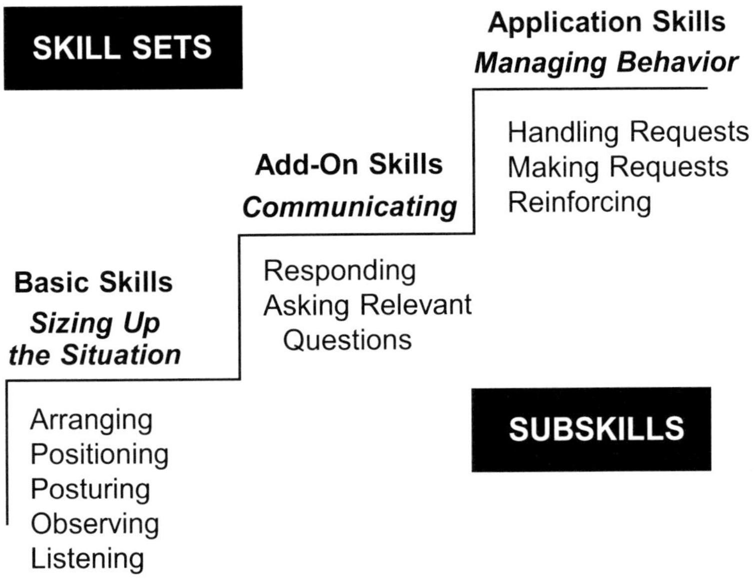

SKILL SETS

Application Skills
Managing Behavior

Handling Requests
Making Requests
Reinforcing

Add-On Skills
Communicating

Responding
Asking Relevant
Questions

Basic Skills
*Sizing Up
the Situation*

SUBSKILLS

Arranging
Positioning
Posturing
Observing
Listening

So, although backed by the rigors of academic research, you will find that the Social Intelligence Skills Model is firmly grounded in common sense. You can expect your instructors to actually use the skills in the classroom as they share them with you.

Obviously, since this is a training program and not counseling or psychotherapy, there is no requirement for you to discuss anything that you may find uncomfortable. In fact, as an added precaution, your instructor will frequently remind you of this so you do not inadvertently share something about which you may later have misgivings.

Remember this is a skills-based training course. The goal of this training is to see that you demonstrate new skills so that you become more adept at managing other people. Only you can choose how and when to apply these new skills.

For example, imagine being confronted by a strong-willed person who has an opposing or critical view of you or of a situation in which you may be involved. Through the effective employment of the **responding skills**, you will be able to summarize the other person's point of view and provide that person with *your* point of view without becoming argumentative. Whether you are dealing with a peer, supervisor, or subordinate, you will be able to gain control of the situation by responding appropriately.

> The ability to effectively employ social intelligence skills ensures that you may choose not to take a passive role. In reality, such skills allow you to increase work quality, productivity, and situational control.

The Skill Sets and
Performance Objectives

The Social Intelligence Skills Model utilized in SoTelligence training consists of skill sets that comprise sub-skills. These skill sets consist of:

- Basic Skills
- Add-On Skills
- Application Skills

Each of these skills sets addresses specific interpersonal proficiencies that have been shown through research to be critical to your performance as a manager. This data will be shared with you during your SoTelligence participation, but for now, let's examine the skill sets and the competencies that they address.

The Basic Skills Set

The Basic Skills Set includes the skills and sub-skills necessary to help you size up situations and people and determine what information you need for successful interaction. This skills set also helps you determine which of the other skills you need to employ in order to get the results you want.

The sub-skills previously shown in Figure 1, such as arranging, positioning, posturing, observing, and listening, seem so obvious and simple that they must be common sense, right? Unfortunately, that is not the case. These nonverbal skills are not only simple and obvious, they have a profound impact on communication. Many social scientists say that accurate communication is actually *at least* up to 70 percent nonverbal. We will look at the research behind this more closely later, but here are a few behaviors that have been identified as necessary for successful interpersonal management that the Basic Skills will help with:

- creates an environment of openness and trust
- gives others undivided attention
- respects others' "personal space"
- faces and maintains appropriate eye contact with others
- conveys interest by maintaining an erect posture
- communicates interest by remaining still while others speak
- accurately observes people, events, and things
- lets others speak without interruption

- listens attentively
- suspends judgment while the other person is speaking.
- interacts with people enough to know and appreciate each one's values
- attends to the surrounding people enough to know the difference between typical behavior and atypical behavior
- recognizes other's emotions
- projects confidence and approachability
- works well with different types of people
- appreciates and understands the importance of diversity
- appears capable and calm under pressure.
- accurately "reads" the nonverbal messages of others

The Add-On Skills Set

The Add-On Skills Set will enhance your communication skills. There are many **interpersonal** (between persons) and **intrapersonal** (within person) uses for this skill set. This skill set is labeled the Add-On Skills Set because it is literally added on to the Basic Skills. These skills will make you a better communicator in social, as well as supervisory, situations. You will be able to establish rapport more effectively, thus enabling you to get better results. In general, the Add-On Skills Set will add to your ability to obtain your objectives. The following specific Add-On Skills Set behaviors have been identified as being important to successful interpersonal interactions:

- seeks input from others and does not interrupt
- clarifies what others are saying to ensure understanding
- creates good "give and take" with others in conversations and meetings
- asks good questions
- encourages suggestions for improvement
- manages his/her own emotions and the emotions of others
- adjusts his/her motivational approach to individual styles/needs
- is respected for fair and effective negotiating
- deals well with resistance
- demonstrates sensitivity to situations that could result in conflict
- accepts criticism well
- maintains calm in high-pressure situations
- respects people's feelings
- finds common ground
- understands the importance of what is NOT said as well as what IS said

- shows concern for others growth and development
- effectively manages crises and stress
- conducts effective group meetings

The Application Skills Set

These skills are directly related to the management of people. Applied with a set of standards, rules, and policies, they will substantially reduce your management difficulties. You are certainly aware of how difficult it is to change the distractive and disruptive people in your life and work environment. Now you will see that there is an **affective** and an **effective** way to manage such people with results favorable to you. Through the use of the Application Skills Set, you can increase the chances of making your point and influence others to listen and act more responsibly. Remember, more skillful management means less stress for you. Following are the desirable Application behaviors sought:

- knows the rules/regulations/policies and applies them fairly
- knows the difference between a request and a demand and when to use each
- investigates all requests to ensure that decisions are based on facts
- provides facts and rationales for requests and decisions
- is an effective negotiator
- introduces needed change even in the face of opposition
- attends to morale when making unpopular decisions
- notifies others of changes or issues that affect them
- is willing to admit when he/she does not know something
- is an effective negotiator and works toward win-win outcomes
- follows through on promises
- distributes time and attention to each person
- helps people see the importance of what they are doing
- holds people accountable for job performance
- provides corrective and positive feedback fairly
- recognizes and rewards people for the work they do
- provides corrective feedback in a professional and respectful manner
- corrects mistakes

SKILL SET OBJECTIVES		
Basic Skills	**Add-On Skills**	**Application Skills**
• Creates an environment of openness and trust • Gives others undivided attention • Respects others' "personal space" • Faces and maintains appropriate eye contact with others • Conveys interest by maintaining an erect posture • Communicates interest by remaining still while others speak • Accurately observes people, events, and things • Lets others speak without interruption • Listens attentively • Suspends judgment while the other person is speaking • Interacts with people enough to know and appreciate each one's values • Attends to the surrounding people enough to know the difference between typical behavior and atypical behavior • Recognizes others' emotions	• Seeks input from others and does not interrupt • Clarifies what others are saying to ensure understanding • Creates good "give and take" with others in conversations and meetings • Asks good questions • Encourages suggestions for improvement • Manages his/her own emotions and the emotions of others • Adjusts his/her motivational approach to individual styles/needs • Is respected for fair and effective negotiating • Deals well with resistance • Demonstrates sensitivity to situations that could result in conflict • Accepts criticism well • Maintains calm in high-pressure situations • Respects people's feelings	• Knows the rules/regulations/policies and applies them fairly • Knows the difference between a request and a demand and when to use each • Investigates all requests to ensure that decisions are based on facts • Provides facts and rationales for requests and decisions • Is an effective negotiator • Introduces needed change even in the face of opposition • Attends to morale when making unpopular decisions • Notifies others of changes or issues that affect them • Is willing to admit when he/she does not know something • Is an effective negotiator and works toward win-win outcomes • Follows through on promises • Distributes time and attention to each person

• Projects confidence and approachability • Works well with different types of people • Appreciates and understands the importance of diversity • Appears capable and calm under pressure • Accurately "reads" the nonverbal messages of others	• Finds common ground • Understands the importance of what is NOT said as well as what IS said • Shows concern for others' growth and development • Effectively manages crises and stress • Conducts effective group meetings	• Helps people see the importance of what they are doing • Holds people accountable for job performance • Provides corrective and positive feedback fairly • Recognizes and rewards people for the work they do • Provides corrective feedback in a professional and respectful manner • corrects mistakes

Exercise 1: The Skill Set Experience

Reflect on a professional life experience where you have been supervised, managed, helped, or supported by someone (It helps to get a mental picture of the person as you do this exercise). In the space below, list the qualities and characteristics of the people whose pictures came into your mind.

_____

_____

_____

_____

_____

_____

_____

_____

_____

_____

_____

_____

The Skill Sets and Performance Objectives Summary

The Social Intelligence Skills Model of the SoTelligence program consists of three skill sets—Basic, Add-On, and Application. These skill sets address specific interpersonal competencies that are essential to your effective performance as a leader, enhancing your ability to be a more effective communicator as well as more effective in establishing rapport and managing more skillfully with less stress. The next three sections will provide an in-depth look at these skills and allow you to practice them in a training setting so that you may begin to experience their benefits first-hand, but first let's examine why training in Social Intelligence is so important.

Why SOCIAL Intelligence?

What IS Intelligence?

What do you think of when you see the word "intelligence"?

Many of us tend to think of "intelligence" as something measured by a test you took in school that resulted in your "IQ" score. For over a century, this has been a common method for us to declare how "smart" we are. But did you know that this test, developed by Alfred Binet (1857–1911), was never intended to measure our intelligence?

At the turn of the 20th century, France was beset with all of the imaginable problems that come with making school attendance compulsory for children aged 6 to 14. Binet was commissioned by the French government in 1899 to develop a method of testing children to determine which ones might have more difficulty performing in the traditional classroom environment and, thus, would need "special education." This work was further developed in 1904 when he and Theodore Simon were commissioned to develop a "mental scale" to further determine children in need of special education.

The "mental scale" consisted of 30 items that could be assigned primarily to three categories:

1. Verbal (Linguistic)
   How well does the child speak? Read? Write? Hear?

2. Quantifiable (Mathematical)
   How well does the child quantify or measure things?

3. Spatial (Visual)
   Is the child able to look at an object or set of objects and determine what Visually fits?

What Binet did NOT intend was to have his scale turn into a measure of intelligence. In separate statements, Binet proclaimed:

"... the scale, properly speaking, does not permit the measure of intelligence, because intellectual qualities are not superposable, and therefore, cannot be measured as linear surfaces are measured." (Gould, 1981)

"Some recent thinkers... [have affirmed] that an individual's intelligence is a fixed quantity; a quantity that cannot be increased. We must protest and react against this brutal pessimism; we must try to demonstrate that it is founded on nothing." (Gould, 1981)

Despite the protests of Binet and others, the Binet-Simon Scale was brought to the United States by American psychologist H. H. Goddard where it was translated into English. Eventually, Stanford University professor Lewis Terman, who believed that intelligence was fixed, standardized the translated version using a large American sample and dramatically changed many of the questions. As the Stanford-Binet Scale, the test was aimed at "curtailing feeble-mindedness. . . and industrial inefficiency." (White, 2000)

Even though there have been voices of caution about the use and abuse of intelligence testing, doesn't it seem logical that those who perform poorly in school will also perform poorly in work? The evidence may surprise you.

Ninety-five Harvard freshmen from the 1940s were assessed 20 years later. On average, those with the highest college test scores were no more happy nor successful in either their private or social lives compared to lower-scoring classmates. They were not more productive; they did not make more money; they did not obtain a higher status. Their satisfaction with life and relationships with friends, family, and significant others were no higher either (Vaillant, 1977).

Arnold (1995) tracked the 1981 Illinois high school valedictorians and salutatorians for a decade. Her findings revealed that only 25% had achieved the highest level of performance and rank in their chosen profession compared to others their age. Her conclusion: getting good grades in school does not predict professional performance or success.

Then there is the Somerville Youth Project (Vaillant and Davis, 2000). Born between 1925 and 1932, 456 economically and educationally disadvantaged sons of immigrant parents living in Somerville, Massachusetts, were studied between 1940 and 1945. Originally assigned as participants in the non-delinquent control group for a longitudinal study on delinquency, they were assessed at the approximate ages of 25, 30, 47, and about every two years after 45. At the age of 60, 349 men were still active in the study.

- 73 (21%) had IQ scores below 87.

    - Nearly half of these men (n = 34) fared as well as men with scores of ≥ 108 (n = 38) in the areas of income, community leadership, and children's education achievement.

    - The ones who "fared well" showed "superior social skills, manual dexterity, and a capacity for rewarding marriages."

        - Social and Emotional skills included the ability to

            - motivate one's self,
            - persist through frustration,

- control impulse and delay gratification,
- manage stress,
- manage one's own feelings, and
- read and deal effectively with the feelings of others.

- Of the 39 with IQ scores below 87 who did not do as well, the strongest predictors for poor outcomes were poor social and emotional competence in childhood and adulthood.

Wagner (2002) said IQ is good for measuring things that

- are well defined,
- are formulated by others,
- come with all the information required to solve the problem,
- have one/several methods for obtaining the correct answer,
- have one correct answer, and
- are unrelated to everyday experience.

The problem is that many real-life/practical problems in diverse careers or personal lives

- are ill defined,
- are formulated without a known solution,
- are missing information essential to the problem's solution,
- may have many possible solutions—each associated with pros and cons,
- have multiple methods to obtain the solution, and
- are related to everyday experience.

If, like Binet, you agree that intelligence is not fixed and intelligence testing is subject to variability, AND you believe that a low IQ score does not necessarily predict low professional performance or personal satisfaction, the question remains: what *IS* intelligence?

This is a question not easily answered as evidenced by the vast numbers of books, journal articles, and websites dedicated to the attempts at answers. Let's start by looking at the word "intelligence."

intell -i- gence

Think	to/through	*Senses*
Talk (i.e., Tell)	*to self through*	*Eyes (See)*
		Ears (Hear)
		Nose (Smell)
		Mouth (Taste)
		Skin (Touch)

I "tell in" or "think to myself" what I sense through my ears, eyes, nose, mouth, and skin.

Then the brain processes, interprets, compartmentalizes, and stores this sensory data.

A portion of our brain that deals with primal emotions (sometimes referred to as the Reptilian Brain) processes the sensations to determine questions like, "Should I get away from here quickly (flight), or should I stay put (fight)?"

These "sensations of the senses" are what we call Feelings.

Our senses can be designated and trained in order for us to get better at processing. This applies to increasing our speed as well as our comprehension.

A key step involved in this consideration of intelligence is the ability to move the sensory data into memory.

Sternberg has proposed a theory of memory that acknowledges the role of our senses (Sternberg, 1997). According to Sternberg, there are three stages:

Stage 1: **Sensory to Mental**
Data comes into the brain through the senses.

Stage 2: **Mental to Mental**
The brain processes the data into meaningful information that can be stored in memory and then accurately and efficiently recalled. This is the process we often use for learning and retaining facts (i.e., "book smart").

Stage 3: **Mental to Sensory**
In this stage, the brain continues to process and analyze the data in ways that allow us to use the new information in novel applications. This, in turn, directs our behaviors. This stage is often referred to as our "Wisdom."

Gardner (1999) suggests that there are *multiple intelligences*, and each *intelligence* may lead to accomplishments in different professional environments. He identified eight dimensions that contain *most* career choices *and* can be studied using a scientific (including neuro-imaging) approach. So,

if you are...	you might consider becoming a...
verbal-linguistic	writer/lawyer/teacher
logical-mathematical	mathematician/economist/doctor
visual-spatial	artist/architect/engineer
bodily-kinesthetic	athlete/dancer/soldier
musical	singer/conductor/disc jockey
naturalistic	scientist/gardener/conservationist
interpersonal	leader/politician/salesperson
intrapersonal	leader/philosopher/psychologist

So, *intelligence* can be a lot of different things based on a lot of different theories, with success measured in many different ways—and all of it sensitive to, but not necessarily determined by, environmental and contextual factors. What the mounting research seems to be revealing is that it is our ***social*** and ***emotional*** abilities that will contribute most to our all-around success in life.

Goleman has written two books on intelligence. In his first, *Emotional Intelligence* (1998), he makes a case for the importance of developing skills in:

1. Self-awareness—What am I feeling? Why? How is it impacting me in this interaction/decision/goal?

2. Self-management—controlling your emotions and adapting to changes in the environment

3. Social awareness—sensing, understanding, and reacting appropriately to others' emotions within complex social environments

4. Relationship management—inspiring, influencing, and developing others while managing conflict

Goleman asserts that our IQ scores have risen 24 points since 1918, and yet our society is plagued by declines in social qualities such as having empathy for others, being able to effectively communicate, developing motivation to reach delayed goals, and establishing lasting interpersonal relationships. In his review of 181 different positions across 121 organizations worldwide, he found that fully two-thirds of the abilities essential to effective performance fell into the categories of social and emotional competencies while the remaining one-third were tied to technical and/or intellectual abilities. Some of his research reviews suggested that the productivity rates of people with social competencies can be equated to "bottom line" measures (e.g., doctors and lawyers are 127 times more productive, and mechanics are 12 times more productive).

Prior to Goleman, Salovey and Mayer (1990) defined emotional intelligence as "the ability to perceive emotion, integrate emotion to facilitate thought, understand emotions, and to regulate emotions to promote personal growth." Since the success of Goleman's book, there has been an increase in the attention and research dedicated to further uncovering and enhancing our knowledge of it.

In Goleman's other book, *Social Intelligence* (2006), he separates the idea of social intelligence from emotional intelligence and asserts that social intelligence is a product of the neural circuitry in the brain—the same circuitry that helps us make and recall memories, make decisions, problem solve, and evaluate situations. By making a move toward establishing social intelligence as a science, it calls into question the idea that social intelligence is the equivalent of "social sense," some mysterious force that some people have, some don't; that some people can develop, some can't; that is crucial for our survival, but unpredictable.

Instead, Goleman speaks of the feelings from our interactions with others that result in biological responses that can affect all of our systems—our hearts, kidneys, lungs, etc. With the help of functional magnetic resonance imaging equipment (MRI), some scientists are tracking the effects of our most stressful relationships on the genes that regulate our immune system. Now, we can literally track the effects of healthy relationships versus toxic ones. Social Neuroscience has helped us discover that our social interactions reshape our brains through neuroplasticity. As Goleman puts it:

> "The social brain represents the **only biological system** in our bodies that continually attunes us to, and in turn becomes influenced by, the internal state of people we're with."

Now, it is important to note that there is a lot of debate among scientists as to just how the results of the fMRI can, or should, be interpreted, and that debate is beyond the scope of this book. Suffice it to say, we are learning more each day with new equipment and new ways of investigating the part our environment plays in shaping our lives and actions.

But for the moment, back to Goleman and some of the highlights, or lowlights, he brings out. American media has brought us stories for years about how we are disconnecting. Forty percent of American two-year-olds spend at least three hours in front of TV daily, and the more TV they watch, the more unruly they get as they age. In 2003, single person households became the most common living arrangement in the United States. The "bystander effect" continues to pervade our interactions with strangers who are in need of our help (i.e., we see someone in need and presume someone else will take care of it—and go about our business).

Putnam, in *Bowling Alone* (2000), sees this as a direct outgrowth of 20 years of steady decline in "social capital." Our lives rarely include a sit down dinner with the rest of the family with no TV, cell phone, texting, etc.

"In the 1970s, two-thirds of Americans belonged to organiza-tions that held regular meetings. This dropped to one-third by the 1990s."

Our technology encourages our interaction disconnect: iPods, cell phones, headphones, e-mail. These devices lead us to connect to the "virtual other" rather than to the flesh and bone person in front of us.

"For every hour spent on the internet, their face-to-face con-tact with friends, coworkers, and family fell by 24 minutes."

Jackson, in *Distracted: The Erosion of Attention and the Coming Dark Age* (2008), echoes these concerns:

"A face to face meeting, which demands a mutual reading of body language, emotion, and soul, is harder to fathom and less predictable than virtual encounter. But by losing the will to face one another, we are turning away from the messy, unpre-dictable, and REAL in life. Virtual pink slips, condolences, courtship, custody visits, lovers' breakups—all relegated the hard parts of life to a thinner, indirect realm."

Now, let's venture back to the setting where this module began: school. According to the Centers for Disease Control and Prevention (CDC), there are approximately 55 million students enrolled in pre-kindergarten through 12th grade. The biggest challenges to their well-being fall across four areas: violence and aggression, alcohol and drug use, attention-deficit/ hyperactivity disorders, and overweight/obesity.

Violence and Aggression

- Youth Violence[1]

  - According to 2005 statistics, an average of 16 people, aged 10–24 years, per day are murdered.

  - Homicide is the second leading cause of death for people aged 10–24 years.

  - In 2006, more than 720,000 people aged 10–24 years were treated for injuries sustained from violence.

- School Violence[2]

  - During the 2005–2006 school year, about 38% of public schools reported at least one incident of violence to law enforcement.

  - Over 25% of students said they were offered, sold, or given an illegal drug on school property in the previous 12 months.

  - Students aged 12 to 18 years were the victims of about 628,200 violent crimes at school, including rape, sexual assault, aggravated assault, and robbery.

  - About 30% of students reported moderate or frequent bullying (13.6% acted as the bully, 10.6% reported being a victim, and 6.3% reported being in both roles).

- Sexual Violence[3, 4]

  - About 8% of high school students report having been forced to have sex.

  - 60.4% of female and 69.2% of male victims were first raped before age 18 years.

  - 25.5% of female and 41.0% of male victims were first raped before the age of 12 years.

---

[1] Centers for Disease Control and Prevention (Summer 2008). Youth violence. www.cdc.gov/injury

[2] Centers for Disease Control and Prevention (2008). School violence fact sheet. www.cdc.gov/injury

[3] Centers for Disease Control and Prevention (2007). Sexual violence fact sheet. www.cdc.gov/injury

[4] Centers for Disease Control and Prevention. (2008). Sexual violence facts at a glance. www.cdc.gov/injury

Attention-Deficit/Hyperactivity Disorders[5, 6]

- Electronic Aggression[7]

    - This is an emerging public health issue and includes acts of threatening, bullying, harassing, and embarrassing others in Internet chat rooms (25%) and on social networking websites (23%). It takes the form of aggressive e-mails (25%), pictures, and instant text messages (16%) to others via computers, cell phones, and other types of technology.

Alcohol and Drug Use[8]

- In 2007, 26% of high school students reported episodic, heavy, or binge drinking.

- 11% of high school students reported they had driven a car while under the influence of alcohol in the previous 30 days.

- 29% of high school students reported riding in a vehicle being driven by someone else in the past 30 days who was under the influence of alcohol.

- Illicit drug use has declined among youth while abuse of over-the-counter (OTC) medications (e.g., cough and cold medications, stimulants, depressants, pain relievers, and tranquilizers) remains high.

Attention-Deficit/Hyperactivity Disorders[9, 10]

- An estimated 4.4 million children aged 4 to 17 years have received a diagnosis of ADD/ADHD.

- Of these, 2.5 million are receiving medication treatment.

---

[5] Centers for Disease Control and Prevention. (10-20-2005). Attention-Deficit/Hyperactivity Disorder (ADHD). www.cdc.gov/ncbddd/adhd/
[6] Centers for Disease Control and Prevention. (10-20-2005). Attention-Deficit/Hyperactivity Disorder (ADHD). www.cdc.gov/ncbddd/adhd/
[7] Centers for Disease Control and Prevention. (01-07-2009). Youth and electronic aggression. www.cdc.gov/features/dsElectronicAggression/
[8] Centers for Disease Control and Prevention. (08-08-2008). Healthy youth! Health topics: Alcohol & drug use. www.cdc.gov/HealthyYouth/alcoholdrug/index/htm
[9] Centers for Disease Control and Prevention. (10-20-2005). Attention-Deficit/Hyperactivity Disorder (ADHD). www.cdc.gov/ncbddd/adhd/
[10] Centers for Disease Control and Prevention. (10-20-2005). Attention-Deficit/Hyperactivity Disorder (ADHD). www.cdc.gov/ncbddd/adhd/

Overweight/Obesity[11, 12]

- Children aged 2 to 5 years—12.4% are considered obese
- Children aged 6 to 11 years—17.0% are considered obese
- Children aged 12 to 19 years—17.6% are considered obese

When we examine the risk factors for alcohol, drug, and violent behaviors, we find that the majority are related to social influences, either directly or indirectly:[13, 14]

- a history of early aggressive behavior
- association with delinquent peers
- involvement in gangs
- poor academic performance
- poor behavioral control
- deficits in social, cognitive, or information-processing abilities
- high emotional distress
- antisocial beliefs and attitudes
- social rejection by peers
- exposure to violence and conflict in the family
- lack of involvement in conventional activities
- harsh, lax, or inconsistent disciplinary practices
- low emotional attachment to parents or caregivers
- poor family functioning/communication
- socially disorganized neighborhoods
- being exposed to social norms that support. . . violence

So having examined some of the evidence for what intelligence *is*, backtracking the evidence for the types of intelligence necessary to live a full and productive life, and facing the evidence of social influences on our children and their futures, we present a model for teaching *skills* in social intelligence—the intelligence for ***intra-*** and ***inter***personal relationships. Because without those relationships, you cannot be successful in the home or the workplace.

---

[11] Centers for Disease Control and Prevention. (11-25-2008). Childhood overweight and obesity. www.cdc.gov/NCCDPHP/DNPA/obesity/childhood/index.htm

[12] Centers for Disease Control and Prevention. (11-25-2008). Overweight and obesity: Obesity prevalence. www.cdc.gov/NCCDPHP/DNPA/obesity/childhood/prealence.htm

[13] Centers for Disease Control and Prevention (2008). School violence fact sheet. www.cdc.gov/injury

[14] Centers for Disease Control and Prevention (2007). Sexual violence fact sheet. www.cdc.gov/injury

But rather than making the reader into a social scientist, our goal is to make you into a *social technologist*.

DIFFERENT PERSPECTIVES

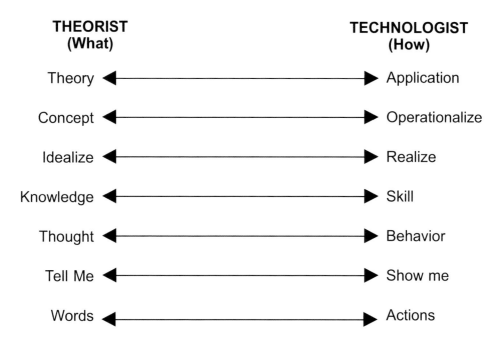

THEORIST (What)		TECHNOLOGIST (How)
Theory	←→	Application
Concept	←→	Operationalize
Idealize	←→	Realize
Knowledge	←→	Skill
Thought	←→	Behavior
Tell Me	←→	Show me
Words	←→	Actions

In a typical learning setting, you would sit in your seat while some "expert" stood in the front of the room, maybe behind a podium, and spoke to you about a topic. They may use a variety of props to add to the lesson (e.g., PowerPoint, videos, handouts), but their primary goal is to use the time to tell you what they know. Let's call this expert a "theorist." This person *tells* you a lot of information about concepts, or ideas, and usually gives you the theory behind the assertions. The theorist talks in terms of the "ideal"—this could be the average or best set of circumstances in which the concept occurs. Overall, the goal of the theorist is to transfer the knowledge and influence the listener's thoughts using spoken and written words by "telling," and the measure of the student's learning is usually by repeating the words back, either through an exam, a paper, or a question-and-answer format. This is an effective way of transmitting knowledge, but does it prepare us to *use* the knowledge? It tells us the "what" but not the "how."

A technologist takes the theory (the "what") to the next level and explains the "how." In other words, the technologist takes the theory and demonstrates how to apply it. The technologist takes the concept and operationalizes it (i.e., defines it in terms that are concrete, behavioral, measureable, and replicable). The technologist takes the concept out of the best-case scenario and places it in real-world scenarios. The technologist takes the knowledge and converts it to skills. To attain proficiency in the skills, the learner must enact specific behaviors. Once the technologist has explained the concept, he/she then models it (i.e., "show me"). Finally, the measure of learning is through the student's actions.

Nobel Prize winning physicist P. T. Bridgman said:

> "The true meaning of a term is to be found by observing what a human does with it, not by what he says about it."

A key component of our explanation is the term "operationalize." This means to explain a concept in ways that are concrete, behavioral, measurable, and replicable (can be duplicated with the same or greatly similar results). To learn how this is done, we are going to do an exercise.

Exercise 2: Five Ways to Operationalize LOVE in the Personal Relationship

1. When buying gas, purchase the person's favorite candy bar and give it to them.

2. Before going to bed, prepare the coffee-maker with his/her special blend, timed to brew when they awake. Next to it, on a linen placemat, place creamer, cinnamon sugar, spoon, linen napkin, and a *real* china cup along with a note: "I appreciate how hard you work. Have a great day!"

3. On the first day of each month, sit down with your loved one and pick three days for a romantic date. Let him/her decide what activities he/she wants to do.

4. Every day, tell the person one specific, unique thing you like about him/her (e.g., "I like it when you laugh really hard").

5. After an argument, say "I'm sorry" before the other person does.

Can you think of one?

After you coach a winning game, when you exit the locker room, I will approach you with a smile & congratulate you & tell you I'm proud of you.

Just as we can operationalize terms in our relationships at home, we can do the same thing for terms in our workplace. Here are some examples of operationalizing the term "respect" in the workplace.

Five Ways to Operationalize
RESPECT in a Leadership Role

1. A subordinate in a meeting says to you, "Why is it so difficult for me to get a meeting with you?" (They've been trying to get a meeting with me for three weeks.) You respond, "Jim, you're entirely right. I'm aware of that. You get with me after the meeting, and we'll set a time."

2. Supervisee Susan Jones walks in your office and appears to have been crying. You get out from behind the desk, ask her to sit in a seat near the desk, sit across from her, and ask her what's wrong.

3. Supervisee John Smith is walking down the hall with his eight-year-old son on "Go to Work with Your Father Day." You see him; he sees you. You observe his son, and you say, "Is this the young man you've been telling me about? Hi, I'm _____, a friend of your dad's *(not 'his BOSS')*." You extend your hand for a handshake and say, "Nice to meet you young man."

4. You're in a meeting that has time constraints, and one of your employees continues to dominate the meeting in terms of his opinions and ignores other people's attempts to communicate their opinions. You decide you need to give other people time and say to the employee, "I appreciate your enthusiasm and your input, but I very much want to get everyone's inputs because of time constraints. I hate to interrupt you, this seems very important to you, and I'd like for you to put some of your ideas in writing and get them to me."

5. You are walking down the hall, and you come upon Susan Johnson and a new employee, Sam Atkins, whom you have not met. Susan walks up to you and wants to introduce you to Sam, and says, "Sam, this is Mr. Gray, the vice president." You extend your hand to Sam, and say, "I prefer to be called Steve. Nice to meet you, sir."

Now, let's review. Human Technology is the study of the techniques for being humane. As such, it involves all dimensions of being human:

- Physical (How to Act)
  How to maintain your physical well-being (i.e., your body)

- Intellectual (How to Think)
  How to think and acquire knowledge

- Social (How to Relate)
  How to relate and maintain your relationships

- Emotional (How to Feel)
  How to maintain your emotional well-being

As Human Technologists, we use skills to demonstrate our knowledge. "Skill" is defined as the ability to know the following:

- Who—person(s) to apply technique(s) with
- What—technique(s) necessary
- When—time to apply the technique(s)
- Where—circumstances to apply the technique(s)
- Why—reason to apply the technique(s)
- How—actions that reflect the technique(s)

For most of us, this is a new way for learning material. To illustrate this, we will make use of Abraham Maslow's concepts *consciousness* and competence as they apply to learning. In developing social intelligence, as with any other skill or behavior, we often don't realize we need the skill or behavior because it has never been brought to our attention *or* we haven't needed the skill before. This is the Unconscious Incompetence Stage. Once we become aware that we need to change, we become defensive about changing—often refusing to modify our behaviors. This is the Conscious Incompetence Stage. But once we decide to make the change and learn the new behavior, we tend to commit to at least trying the new behavior or skill a few times. And for most of us, the first few times we try a new behavior, it feels uncomfortable and unnatural. This is the Conscious Competence Stage. But if we persist, eventually, the new behavior is a natural part of our behaviors. We don't even think about it before we use. It is second nature. When this occurs, we say we have achieved Unconscious Competence. This model of competency is presented on the following page.

UNSKILLED		
↓	**_Unconscious Incompetence_**	Don't know change is needed
	Conscious Incompetence	Defensive to change/ modify behavior
	Conscious Competence	Mechanics/new behavior
HIGHLY SKILLED	**_Unconscious Competence_**	Fluid/non-mechanical behavior (response generalized)

The more you practice, the less mechanical and more natural a new behavior (or skills) feels. For those of you who resist putting these skills into play because they feel "too mechanical," we can't resist quoting our mentor, Dr. John D. Blakeman:

> *"I'd rather you be mechanically helpful
> than spontaneously harmful."*

Now some of you may question a need to change. You may say, "Hey, this is just who I am. Love me, or leave me. I can't change. It's my *nature*." To that, we say there is a lot of research on just what is attributable to your genetic heritage (your heredity). This table shows the personality trait in the left column and the percentage of the extent to which heredity is responsible for that trait in the right column (Bouchard and McGuire, 2003).

Personality Trait	Heritability Estimate
General cognitive ability	50%
Extroversion	54%
Agreeableness	42%
Conscientiousness	49%
Neuroticism	48%
Openness	57%
Aggression	38%
Traditionalism	54%

To date, we have not found a single personality trait that is 100% determined by your genetics. Therefore, no matter what the trait is that you want to change, it's possible. And social and environmental influences are powerful as we briefly discussed in the Intelligence module.

If you are still reading this, the chances are that we have at least piqued your interest in becoming a Human Technologist in order to improve your *intra-* and *inter*personal interactions as a leader, a friend, a family member, and/or a citizen. Great! That means you're ready to begin your skills training.

But first, we want to talk about the most basic, but essential, component of any relationship—communication. At the root of every relationship lies the ability to accurately and effectively communicate with another person or group of people. And communication consists of lots of things, but primarily it can be broken down into two categories: nonverbal and verbal. Before you skip forward to the "How to Respond" section, we'd like to talk about the power of nonverbal communication.

The Mehrabian Communications Model posits this statistic that is widely accepted among communication experts.

In effect, spoken communication is:

- 7% of the meaning comes from the verbal message,

- 38% of the meaning comes from the paralanguage (tone, volume, accent, pause, etc.), and

- 55% of the meaning comes from the facial expression.

(http://businessballs.com/mehrabiancommunications.htm)

Other research asserts a more modest role for nonverbal communication. These studies indicate that nonverbal behaviors account for 60—70% of the variance in our daily and work communications.

Understanding Nonverbal Variance in Communication (60–70% of the Variance)

- **Arranging (environmental factors)**
  - Physical setting
  - Social rules
  - Cultural factors

- **Positioning (body placement; proxemics)**
  - Proximity
    - Squared/angled/side-by-side/behind
  - Distancing
    - Social—5'–10'
    - Personal—3'–5'
    - Intimate—0'–3'

- **Posturing (body erectness; kinesics)**
  - Standing/sitting erect
  - Leaning forward

- **Gesturing**
  - Hands, feet, legs, arm movement

- **Paralanguage (voice)**
  - Tones/inflection/volume/pauses/accents/speed
  - Direct link to emotional state of the speaker

- **Facing**
  - Eye (movement/contact)
  - Mouth (how one holds their mouth—open/closed)
  - Facial muscles (emotional state of person: meanings are *universal*)

- **Touching (haptics)**
  - Ten times more powerful than verbal
  - Where/how/when is contextually determined
  - Social appropriateness

- **Appearance**
  - Height/weight/gender/age/race/grooming/dress

Module 2: The Science Behind Nonverbal Communication

The Science Behind
Nonverbal Communication

As was mentioned earlier, the Mehrabian Communications Model suggests that over half of the meaning of a spoken message comes from our facial expressions while more than a third comes from our paralanguage. But this model does not generalize to every communication situation. Telephone conversations exclude facial expressions, but that doesn't mean we know how that 55% of the variance is redistributed. E-mail excludes facial expressions *and* paralanguage, but does that mean that 93% of the message is guaranteed to be lost (http://businessballs.com/mehrabiancommunications.htm)? What we do know is that, without facial expression, there is a greater likelihood that the communication may be inaccurately interpreted.

And so, it is important that we take this opportunity to review a few of the studies related to our model. The following studies done in the area of nonverbal communication are not intended to be an exhaustive literature review. In fact, they are presented as short outcomes rather than as a thesis into the science of social interactions. Our intent is simply to provide you with some background and insight into some of the types of studies being conducted and some of the outcomes especially pertinent to our subject matter. In the back of this book, you will find an extensive list of References that have been included throughout this manual along with a Recommended Readings List. If you would like more information on any of these topics, these lists can provide you with some stepping-stones into more in-depth reviews.

Arranging (Environmental Factors)

- Physical setting
- Social rules
- Cultural factors

Arranging involves managing the physical setting to invite interaction. This can include arranging the physical space (e.g., moving furniture, adding soft lighting, removing distractions) as well as knowing the social and cultural rules of the setting. This, by default, includes having an understanding of the people present in the environment.

Physicians in exam rooms with no desk, no height difference compared to the patient, and an interactional space of three feet or less exhibited greater eye contact and touch compared to physicians in an exam room with a desk, standing over the patient, and standing/ sitting more than three feet away (Gorawara-Bhat et al., 2007).

Lee and Wagner (2002) found that adult women who were asked to talk about a positive experience and a negative experience were less likely to discuss their emotional states when an experimenter was present. While discussing their experiences with the experimenter present, they smiled more overall, and they were more likely to display positive emotions when discussing *both* the positive and the negative experiences. The only time there was congruence between the facial display and the emotion being disclosed was when the woman was alone, and the emotion was positive.

When shown photographs of college employees interacting with one another, the majority of undergraduates were able to determine with a high degree of accuracy who was "the boss" and who was "the employee" (Mast and Hall, 2004).

When shown silent film clips of couples interacting, people who have declared themselves as "in love" tended to detect love among the filmed couples more often than it actually appeared—and they were more confident in their judgments compared to individuals who were currently not in a relationship (Aloni and Bernieri, 2004).

Friends tend to be more accurate than strangers at identifying our emotion states when judging us purely on our nonverbal cues; however, our closest friends are not the best judges of our concealed emotional states of sadness and anger. That honor is best performed by our more distant friends and acquaintances (Sternglanz and DePaulo, 2004).

We tend to be a better judge of emotional expression when judging cultures that are far different from our own—especially if we receive immediate feedback (Elfenbein, 2006). This could be due to the novelty of the experience of observing a different culture.

Naturalistic observation studies of college-age heterosexual Hispanic and Asian couples revealed that interactants from "contact" cultures (in this case, Hispanic) were more likely to embrace in public, and interactants from "non-contact" cultures (in this case, Asian) were less likely to touch in public (Regan et al., 1999).

As a group, Czech men display more hand touches than Italian men, Italian women, American men, or American women. Czech men along with Italian men and Italian women displayed more nonhand touches than any other group (DiBaise and Gunnoe, 2004).

One study found that undergraduates exposed to interparental violence throughout their lives were significantly less able to correctly interpret "happy" nonverbal cues in others (Hodgins and Belch, 2000). Contrary to popular media portrayals, they were not more successful in recognizing "anger" or "fear" in others compared to undergraduates who had not experienced interparental violence. When the two groups were compared, everyone consistently displayed congruent nonverbal cues with their own posed emotion.

Positioning (Body Placement; Proxemics)

- Proximity
  - Squared/angled/side-by-side/behind
- Distancing
  - Social—5'-10'
  - Personal—3'-5'
  - Intimate—0'-3'

We know that personal space, as a measure, differs cross-culturally, and it expands and contracts contextually (Hogh-Olesen, 2008). Personal space can get re-defined when you enter a space where someone else already is or someone enters your space.

In a field study of adolescent group behaviors, Terneus and Malone (2004) observed

- in dual gender groups, females tended to stand on one side of the circle and males tended to stand on the other side;
- when a female left the group and did not immediately return to the group, the group disbanded;
- if a male left the group, his "spot" remained vacant while the group interaction continued; and
- the reasons for group disbanding were (1) females talked exclusively or excessively to other females, (2) a female left, flipped her hair, and did not immediately return, (3) a female claimed a position between two males, (4) and a female displayed an aggressive behavior toward a male by stepping into his intimate space.

After the groups disbanded, only the males accurately identified the behaviors that occurred as the groups disbanded (i.e., that all groups disbanded after a female action occurred). None of the females could give an explanation for how or why the group disbanded. Females displayed the following behaviors in the groups: taking the model stance, swaying within hip radius, turning the torso at the waist to attend to a male, turning the torso and leaning to attend to females, showing the palm of the hand, making slight hand and limb gestures restricted within the range of the hips, primping hair, smoothing clothing, nodding, tossing the head, hair flipping, scanning the group visually, darting glances at a specific person in the group, gazing directly at a specific person in the group, coyly smiling with a downward gaze, smiling with or without showing teeth, giggling, and licking lips. Male behaviors included standing straight with either arms crossed or straight down by their sides, shrugging, rocking, turning the head 90° to attend to a female, head tossing, nodding, smiling faintly, laughing with other males in the group, scanning the group as well as outside the group, and darting glances at a specific person either inside or outside of the group. Faux pas behaviors included stepping outside of the group and not immediately returning, hair flipping, brushing, pointing, talking and/or laughing excessively or exclusively with like gendered others. The females displayed astonished and confused facial expressions when a male left the group (Terneus and Malone, 2004).

Ray and Floyd (2006) found that "behaviors related to pleasantness, involvement, immediacy, and positivity (including proximity, smiling, gaze, and vocal pitch variation) were consistently observed in communicators who were judged as likeable."

Posturing (Body Erectness; Kinesics)

- Standing/sitting erect
- Leaning forward

Darwin conducted some of the earliest scientific observations about posturing, studying head positioning and the expansion and contraction of the chest as nonverbal signals for communicating emotion (as cited in Keltner and Shiota, 2003).

A constricted posture is indicative of embarrassment and/or shame while an expansive posture is associated with boasting and/or pride (Keltner and Shiota, 2003).

A raised head is more often associated with dominance and "superiority" emotions such as contempt and pride, whereas a lowered or tilted head is generally perceived as submissive and associated with sadness and "inferiority" emotions such as shame, embarrassment, guilt, and humiliation (Mignault and Chaudhuri, 2003).

Women are better at determining the mood associated with a particular sitting or standing posture compared to men. People who are trained in the use of their bodies (e.g., dancers) are more accurate when determining mood of sitting or standing postures (Pitterman and Norwicki, 2004). Similarly, restaurant managers who were better at correctly identifying the moods associated with sitting and standing postures were rated higher by coworkers in the areas of empathy and caring (Byron, 2002). Sales professionals assessed for their ability to correctly identify moods through postures revealed that those who had fewer errors also had higher sales and salaries. Errors that resulted in mistaking anger as fear and fear as sadness were the most predictive (Teranova, 2002).

Gesturing

- Hands, feet, legs, arm movement

Nonverbal behaviors play a role in our memory processing. Three groups (7- to 8-year-olds, 9- to 10-year-olds, and a group of adults) watched film clips of a conversation exercise where the gestures did not match the verbal message. The 9- to 10-year-olds were unable to process *both* the verbal and nonverbal behaviors. They could recall one or the other accurately, but not both; whereas, the 7- to 8-year-olds and the adults had no problem recalling both the verbal and the nonverbal behaviors (Church, Kelly, and Lynch, 2000).

Paralanguage (Voice)

- Tones/inflection/volume/pauses/accents/speed
- Direct link to emotional state of the speaker

"Paralanguage refers to the wide variety of vocal behaviors that occur in speech but that are not part of the sound system of language, as traditionally conceived" (Duncan, 1972).

Laughter appears to help regulate the flow of conversations and interactions, and it is often self-initiated rather than elicited from external sources. As such it acts to mitigate the meaning of the verbiage that preceded it (Vettine and Todt, 2004).

More varied pitch was found to be an indicator of "liking" only in females. Males experienced varied pitch as less than positive. When talking to a person we like, we tend to decrease our volume over time as well as the amount of time we talk—possibly to increase our attending time. However, these same behaviors may communicate a desire to disengage (Ray and Floyd, 2006).

Balge and Milner (2000) found that mothers more likely to abuse a child were those who made more errors in accurately identifying a child's emotions through voice cues.

Sex offenders make more errors in recognizing angry voice tones compared to other groups (Mitchell, 2001).

An adult who is able to correctly identify a child's emotions based on his/her voice is likely to be more socially adjusted and competent (Rothman and Nowicki, 2004).

Heilveil and Muehleman (1981) found that the length of a response, errors in speech and/or grammar, and hesitation before answering questions were associated with perceived lying.

Facing

- Eye (movement/contact)
- Mouth (how one holds their mouth—open/closed)
- Facial muscles (emotional state of person: meanings are *universal*)

One of the most heavily researched areas of emotion is related to the display and recognition of emotions via facial expressions. Ekman's *Emotions Revealed* (2003) is the ultimate and seminal culmination of his long-standing research into the area, and it has provided the "jumping off" point for hundreds of other studies. Expressions are more personal than speech because they communicate our feelings. For instance, the human smile is visible for long distances.

One debate in the area of facial expressions has been over the purpose of facial displays: are they for expressing emotions, behavioral intentions, or action requests? Horstmann (2003) conducted a series of studies in which the results consistently pointed to the use of facial displays to determine emotions. As such, we seem to be better at identifying complex facial expressions compared to singular facial expressions (LaPLante and Ambady, 2000).

Kohler et al. (2004) found that the physiological cues that make up a facial display of emotion are not always the ones associated with the recognition of that emotion (see Table 1).

Heisel and Mongrain (2004) examined the effects of conflict between romantic couples on facial expressions. Highly ambivalent women (as measured by the Ambivalence over the Expression of Emotion Questionnaire) showed a greater number of negative facial expressions and a shorter duration of positive expressions compared to women with lower levels of measured ambivalence. The number of negative facial expressions in women predicted dysphoria and mild anxiety in their male partners.

A few studies have used a technique of creating matched male and female photographs using a single androgynous facial expression surrounded by either a male or female hairline. Using this technique, Hess et al. (2004) found that anger displays were more often accurately decoded when displayed by an apparent woman compared to an apparent man. Anger expressions were rated more intense when observed in apparent women compared to apparent men. Happiness was rated as more intense when identified in apparent men. Overall, apparent women were perceived as more often displaying anger, and apparent men were more often perceived as displaying apparent happiness and surprise.

Table 1. Comparison of Physical Cues to Recognition Cues

Emotion	Physical Cues	Recognition Cues
Happy	• Raised inner eyebrows • Tightened lower eyelid • Raised upper lip • Lip corners turned upward	• Raised cheeks • Lid tightening • Raised outer brow
Sad	• Furrowed eyebrow • Open mouth with upper lip raised • Lip corners stretched and turned down • Chin pulled up	• Lowered eyebrow • Raised cheek
Anger	• Lowered eyebrows • Eyes wide open with tightened lower lid • Lips exposing teeth and stretched lip corners	• Lowered eyebrows • Raised upper lids • Lower lip depression
Fear	• Eyes wide open • Furrowed and raised eyebrows • Stretched mouth	• Raised upper lip • Nostril dilation • Raised inner eyebrow • Widened eyes

Utilizing chimeric photographs (i.e., a photograph of two left hemispheres pasted together to create a full face image or a photograph of two right hemispheres pasted together to create a full face image), Indersmitten, and Gur (2003) found that the emotions of posed fear, provoked fear, posed sadness, provoked sadness, posed happiness, provoked happiness, and posed anger are expressed more intensely in the left hemisphere of the face (or hemiface), while provoked anger is expressed more intensely in the right hemiface. In contrast to the emotional intensity levels demonstrated by the left hemiface, the right hemiface expresses emotions more efficiently and accurately. This suggests that there might be two different neural substrates associated with facial displays of emotion. Provoked anger is expressed more intensely *and* more accurately in the right hemiface, and this information is processed by the right side of the viewer's brain which is also the dominant site for emotion recognition. This was supported, in part, by Davidson et al. (2004) who discovered that we have more facial movement in the left side of our face when we express sadness compared to our expressions of happiness.

The Duchenne smile (smiling with both corners of the mouth pulled up and the muscle that orbits the eye is active) is a reliable indicator of enjoyment and pleasant compared to smiling that does not include the muscle that orbits the eye (Ekman et al., 1990). And appearing happy can be beneficial to your interpersonal health. One study found that people wearing facial expressions of happiness and surprise were perceived as high in dominance and affiliation. Those displaying anger were perceived as high in dominance and low in affiliation, and those displaying sadness and fear were perceived as low in dominance (Montepare and Dobish, 2003).

Age is another factor in identifying facial expressions. Three-, four-, and five-year-olds watched a film of a person taking a drink and then saying, "I like it," while displaying an inconsistent facial expression (such as frowning). When the inconsistency between the verbal statement and the facial expression was exaggerated, the children tended to rely on the facial expression to determine if the actor liked the beverage. When the inconsistency was not as obvious, the children relied on the verbal message (Eskritt and Lee, 2003).

Children with learning disabilities have significantly more trouble in the perception of facial expression cues compared to children who were learning disabled *with* attention-deficit/hyperactivity disorder or children who had no disorder (Sprouse et al., 1998). Likewise, children (8 to 12) in a heightened state of social anxiety generally ascribed emotions more often to photos of neutral faces and took longer to identify emotions compared to less socially anxious children of the same age (Melfsen and Florin, 2002).

Sullivan and Ruffman (2004) studied healthy elderly adults and found them to be significantly impaired when asked to identify anger and sadness, but they were very adept at identifying fear and happiness. When shown two photographs of varying intensity levels of the same emotion, they were significantly impaired judging which was the most intense expression of angry, sad, or fearful, but they performed well identifying the most intensely happy or disgusting face.

When asked to observe film clips of individuals giving incongruent messages (i.e., the verbal message did not match the facial expression), one group of older adults (mean age = 77) had difficulty differentiating between levels of intensity among emotions. When recounting the verbal message, they tended to change the verbal message to match the observed facial expression (Thompson, et al., 2001).

Mood also affects our abilities to accurately identify facial expressions. Individuals scoring high on the Cook-Medley Hostility Scale were more likely than low-scoring individuals to inaccurately identify expressions of disgust as anger and expressions of happiness as neutral. Males more often identified disgust and anger compared to females (Larkin et al., 2002). In a study of depressed patients, Leppanen et al. (2004) found that both depressed and non-depressed individuals were equally accurate in identifying happy and sad faces. However, while the non-depressed group identified neutral faces equally as well as happy and sad faces, the depressed group was significantly less accurate identifying neutral faces. Depressed patients also took longer to identify neutral faces. Overwhelmingly, depressed individuals interpreted neutral faces as either sad or happy. This tendency toward misidentification of facial expressions persisted even after depression symptoms were judged to be in remission.

Individuals who are prone to anxiety tend to judge ambiguous information as more threatening (Eubank, et al., 2002).

Adults in a heightened state of social anxiety take longer to identify facial expressions in others; however, they do not make more errors compared to others in a less stressful state (Mullins and Duke, 2004).

Psychological disorders can also interfere with our ability to accurately identify facial expressions. A study of Japanese and French paranoid schizophrenics revealed a significantly lower ability to accurately recognize hatred and an even more impaired ability to recognize fear compared to non-paranoid schizophrenics, regardless of cultural background (Okada et al., 2003).

Chemicals can affect our recognition of facial expressions. Diazepam inhibited participants' abilities to accurately identify expressions of fear and anger but not of other emotions; however, Metoprolol did not have any measurable effect. The errors related to Diazepam were primarily mistaking fear for surprise and disgust for anger (Zangara et al., 2002).

Studies of alcohol dependence and facial expression recognition consistently reveal an impairment for processing facial cues. Foisy et al. (2005) found that past opiate-dependent individuals who were also recovering alcoholics were less able to accurately identify expressions compared to past opiate-dependent individuals, regardless of how long the recovering alcoholic had abstained from ingesting alcohol. Both groups were significantly inhibited in their ability to recognize emotions. Kornreich et al. (2002) also found that recovering alcoholics performed much poorer when attempting to identify happiness, anger, sadness, and disgust, and, when asked how well they thought they did with the identification process, they were unaware of their decoding errors. The same study revealed that the recovering alcoholics also reported more interpersonal problems in the areas of assertiveness, sociability, submissiveness, intimacy, and taking too much responsibility. In fact, the more interpersonal problems a recovering alcoholic experienced, the less able he/she was to accurately identify a facial expression. Finally, Townshend and Duka (2003) tested detoxing alcoholics compared to social drinkers using photographs of faces displaying two expressions. The results of this study indicated that the detoxing alcoholics consistently overestimated the presence and intensity of fear while demonstrating different patterns for recognizing anger and disgust when compared to the social drinkers. Additionally, the more previous detoxifications the individual had experienced, the less accurate they were with their identifications.

Traumatic Brain Injury (TBI) and/or brain disease that results in a bilaterally damaged amygdala results in an inability to accurately identify facial expressions of fear compared to non-amygdala-damaged controls. Additionally, amygdala damaged individuals tend to exhibit higher rates of confusion when rating fear/anger and happiness (Sato et al., 2002).

Touching (Haptics)

- Ten times more powerful than verbal
- Where/how/when is contextually determined
- Social appropriateness

Haptics is the study of patterns of tactile interactions (Austin as cited in Duncan, 1969), while tactile communication occurs "when there are systematic changes in another's perceptions, thoughts, feelings, or behavior as a function of another's touch in relation to the context in which it occurs" (Hertenstein, 2002). Darwin proposed that touching was a universal way of expressing intimacy across species, including humans (as cited in Keltner and Shiota, 2003).

Touch is the most developed sense at birth (Hertenstein et al., 2006). It is one of the strongest forms of pre-verbal communication. Even so, research around the sense of touch remains sparse compared to the other senses. The paucity of research is accounted for, in part, by (1) strong desires by researchers to investigate the "more important" and/or "noble" sense of vision and hearing, (2) the fact that touch takes place in private and is hard to access, (3) the complexity of touch (e.g., one study identified over 475 types of touching), and (4) social rules, mores, and taboos make the study of touch difficult in a laboratory situation.

In a study of male university employees and harassment in the workplace, more than half indicated they had experienced gender harassment, 20% indicated they had experienced seductive behaviors perpetrated by a female, but the most cited inappropriate behavior (chosen from a list) was "unwelcome touching on the arm" (Gerrity, 2000).

Individuals with body dysmorphic disorder tend to display self-touching behaviors of the "affected" area along with excessive grooming, excessive changes of clothing, mirror checking, and camouflaging the "defect" (Phillips et al., 2008).

In a dyad role play, one person was assigned the role of art gallery owner while the other was designated as the owner's assistant. After the interaction, each was asked to recall the other's hand gestures, self-touch, gazing, smiling, and nodding. There were no significant differences between the two in the accuracy of their recall *except* the assistants were more accurate recalling the owners' self-touch behaviors (Hall, et al., 2001).

Kneidinger et al. (2001) observed various athletic teams under game conditions and reported that females performed more touching behaviors compared to males; males performed touching behaviors more frequently at away games versus home games; females performed touching behaviors more frequently at home games versus away games; and females performed touching behaviors more frequently after events with negative outcomes compared to males.

Preschool children with high levels of aggressive behaviors received therapeutic massages for 5 to 10 minutes and/or extra attention daily. After three months, those children receiving massage and/or extra attention showed marked decreases in their aggressive behavior; however, after six months, only the children who received massage, either alone or combined with extra attention, were maintaining their decreased levels of aggression. Parents indicated that these children were sleeping more peacefully and for longer periods of time (von Knorring et al., 2008).

Infants (5½-months-old) were observed interacting with their mothers when the mothers were interactive and expressive compared to when the mothers displayed a still, neutral face. When mothers were interactive and expressive, the infants used passive touch (laying a hand in one place and leaving it there), and they spent significantly more time touching their mothers. When the mothers were non-expressive and still, the infants used more active, soothing, reactive touches (like stroking, fingering, patting, and pulling), and they spent more time touching themselves. Moszkowski and Stack (2007) suggest that this indicates an infant's desire to communicate affective states through touch.

Appearance

- Height/weight/gender/age/race/grooming/dress

The best research review for this section comes from our daily lives. It seems to be human nature that we make judgments based on appearance. Reality TV captures the harassment and mistreatment of models wearing "fat suits" and a hidden camera on a New York subway. One of the most popular shows on television, "Ugly Betty," is about a plain, mismatched clothed young lady with a home haircut and braces who surprises the fashion industry with her abilities and sensibility. News stories are replete with accounts of everyday citizens being targeted for scrutiny based on how they look, dress, or talk. All of us, it seems, have hidden implicit attitudes (i.e., biases) regarding some (or maybe many) appearance factors. One of the best ways to discover your implicit attitudes is to participate in a Harvard study, https:// implicit.harvard.edu/implicit/. This site will not only provide you with the opportunity to uncover your hidden prejudices, you will be contributing to a growing area of research. One of the best results from this research thus far: we *can* change our attitude through education and interaction with groups about whom we have preconceived notions.

Having said that, we could not resist presenting a couple of research outcomes. For instance, did you know that when a woman makes eye contact with a man who finds her very attractive, dopamine is released in *his* brain, and he feels pleasure.

Women who appear to be pregnant are met with more hostility as job applicants by both male and female employees compared to non-pregnant women. The hostility increases significantly if the job the pregnant woman is applying for is considered "typically male" (Hebl et al., 2007).

Fourteen children between 36- and 72-months-old were observed in the presence of a robotic dog and then in the presence of a real dog. Nearly one-third of the children refused to participate in the session with the robotic dog, while 18% of the children refused to participate in the session with the live dog. Children initiated approaching the robotic dog more than they initiated approaching the real dog; they interacted with the robotic dog more than the real dog; they touched the robotic dog more than the real dog, they laughed while playing with the robotic dog more than the real dog. Nevertheless, 71% of the children indicated they preferred the live dog while only one child said he preferred the robotic dog (Ribi et al., 2008).

What we've just reviewed is literally the tip of the nonverbal communication iceberg. Considering all of the variability that goes into our interactions, is it any wonder that we are often misunderstood?

Know Thyself
(*Intra*personal Intelligence)

Just how accurate is *your* judgment of your interpersonal abilities compared to what your friends, family, and colleagues think?

Dunning (2005) found that, most of the time, our perceptions and judgments about ourselves do not match up well with those of our family, friends, and work associates. Many of the correlational studies revealed no relationship between various factors. Remember, correlations measure the relationship between two things. They can be positive—the two things being compared increase together (e.g., as we get taller, our weight increases) or negative—of the two things being compared, one increases while the other decreases (e.g., when pain medication dosage is increased, the experience of pain decreases). Correlation values range from +1 to −1. In human behavior research, a correlation of 0 to .1 is considered a nonexistent relationship; a 0.2 to 0.3 is considered weak, a 0.4 to 0.5 is considered moderate, and a 0.6 or higher is considered strong. For example, the correlation between gender and height is 0.7. Here are some of Dunning's findings:

- IQ test prediction of our ability to accurately judge ourselves = 0.2 to 0.3

- Freshman student perception of academic performance vs. instructors perceptions = 0.35

- Workplace performance: how people expect to perform vs. how they actually do = 0.20

- Interpersonal skills (how others see you vs. how you see yourself) = 0.17

- Managerial competence (how we see ourselves vs. how others see us) = .04

- How an athlete sees his/her performance vs. how the coaches and others see his/her performance = 0.47

Why do you think the athlete is so much more attuned to his/her per-formance?

Athletes get instant feedback when they do something wrong (or right!). The fans boo or cheer, the coach provides immediate feedback, the teammates provide immediate feedback, the score provides feedback, their performances are replayed on the big screen at the park or the small screen back at training camp. They are bombarded with feedback.

That is not the way most of us experience our lives.

Dunning points out that an outsider's perspective tends to be "constant," "immediate," and "unambiguous," while the complex social interaction (which characterizes most interpersonal interactions) tends to be occasional, often delayed, and ambiguous. Is it any wonder why there is such a disconnect between how we see ourselves and how others see us?

We've taken a lot of time and covered a lot of information to build a foundation for understanding the importance of this training as well as how this training may be different from other courses or books you may have been exposed to. This training will affect the actions and exchanges that are at the core of every interaction you have with others—and with yourself. So, without further delay, let's get started.

Module 3: The Basic Skills Set

Sizing up the Situation

The Basic Skills Set comprises communication skills that are often assumed and taken for granted. Many of these skills and sub-skills may appear to be common sense—everyone knows how to look at the person with whom they are communicating and how to listen to others. Or do we? As mentioned earlier in the research data section, we often do not see (or hear) what is really going on. We must put aside what we have long taken for granted and begin to listen and look anew. The Basic Skills Set, consisting of arranging, positioning, posturing, observing, and listening skills as well as their sub-skills, will assist you in looking at these routine behaviors in a different light. The implementation of these skills will greatly improve your interpersonal communication by helping you *size up the situation*.

Figure 2. The Basic Skills: Sizing Up the Situation

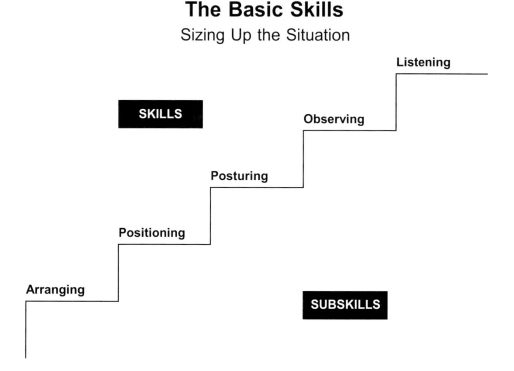

The Basic Skills
Sizing Up the Situation

Arranging

Entire industries have developed around the concept of arranging the environment in order to increase sales (think home staging, decorating, or product placement in stores and movies), influence mood and energy (Feng shui), and direct or assist human and animal behaviors (e.g., orienting all of the furniture around the TV).

How you arrange or order the environment in which you manage or live contributes to your goal achievement. If you are highly skilled regarding your interpersonal management skills, the arrangement of the environment will be somewhat overshadowed in importance by your skill level. However, if you regard your people management skills as only moderately effective, as is the case with most of us, then this is an area where you should expend real effort.

Pretend for a moment that you have had a conflict with someone at home this morning. When you get home tonight, what room in your residence would you pick to meet in to deal with the conflict? Why?

Your environment is a variable in shaping your behavior, and when you are arranging the environment for interactions with others, your environment becomes a *precision decision*.

Sometimes the person under stress needs to pick the room to have the discussion in.

When we examine the behaviors of highly functional "professionals," one dominant characteristic of their personality is that they place a lot of significance and importance on details. Arranging sub-skills focuses on the details of the environment.

Arranging is the first skill of the Basic Skills Set. *Arranging* means eliminating from the environment anything that might distract you or the person whom you are supervising or with whom you are interacting. A dual goal is to make the environment pleasant, not stressful. The sub-skills of arranging are listed in Figure 3.

Figure 3. The Basic Skills: Arranging

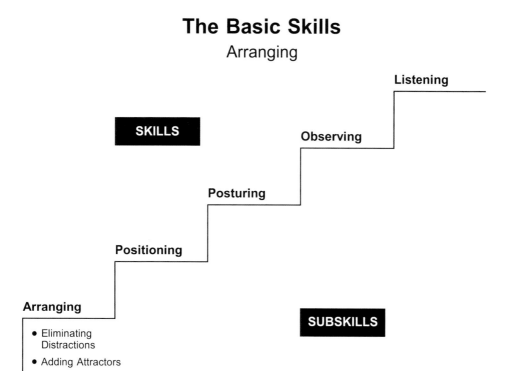

The Basic Skills
Arranging

Listening

SKILLS

Observing

Posturing

Positioning

Arranging

- Eliminating Distractions
- Adding Attractors

SUBSKILLS

The Sub-Skills of Arranging

Eliminating Distractions. The first sub-skill of arranging is *eliminating distractions*. Most people have worked in an environment where there were many distractions. Remember what it was like to try to perform your job effectively when you worked in a distracting environment? Extraneous noises, uncomfortable chairs, and an uncomfortable room temperature can deter one's attention and deplete one's energy so that more time is required for each task and errors are more frequent.

Imagine the work environment in which you manage. Are there noises that can be eliminated? Can phone calls be intercepted? Is furniture reasonably comfortable? Does the placement of furniture create an undesirable barrier? Or is it best to simply remove yourself and the person with whom you are talking from the distracting work environment, and talk with him or her in a quiet conference room? Eliminating those distractions is important to successful communications.

Exercise 3: Eliminating Distractions

List some distractions you have experienced when you have been in a supervisor's presence and communication was important.

1. _____

2. _____

3. _____

Adding Attractions. The second sub-skill of arranging is *adding attractions.* Following the elimination of the distractions, you might consider actually adding attractions to the environment. You can enhance your work environment in order to manage (communicate) more effectively. Providing privacy, comfortable furniture, eliminating barriers and having refreshments may all facilitate your efforts. Your best standard is probably the one you would establish for yourself.

Exercise 4: Adding Attractions

List some characteristics in your work environment that contribute to either reducing your stress or to facilitating your communication with others.

1. _____

2. _____

3. _____

Positioning

Positioning is the second skill of the Basic Skills Set. *Positioning* means placing your body so that you are able to observe, listen, or perform some physical act. If your goal is to get information, manage, or help others, it makes sense to prepare yourself in order to achieve the goal you have in mind. Do not regard the discussion and practice of positioning as being unworthy of consideration. Examine the importance of proper positioning in other activities such as sports activities, surgery, music, etc. If you accept the premise that there are skills involved in interpersonal transaction, then the Basic Skills become important to the process of communication. The sub-skills of positioning are listed in Figure 4.

Figure 4. The Basic Skills: Positioning

The Basic Skills
Positioning

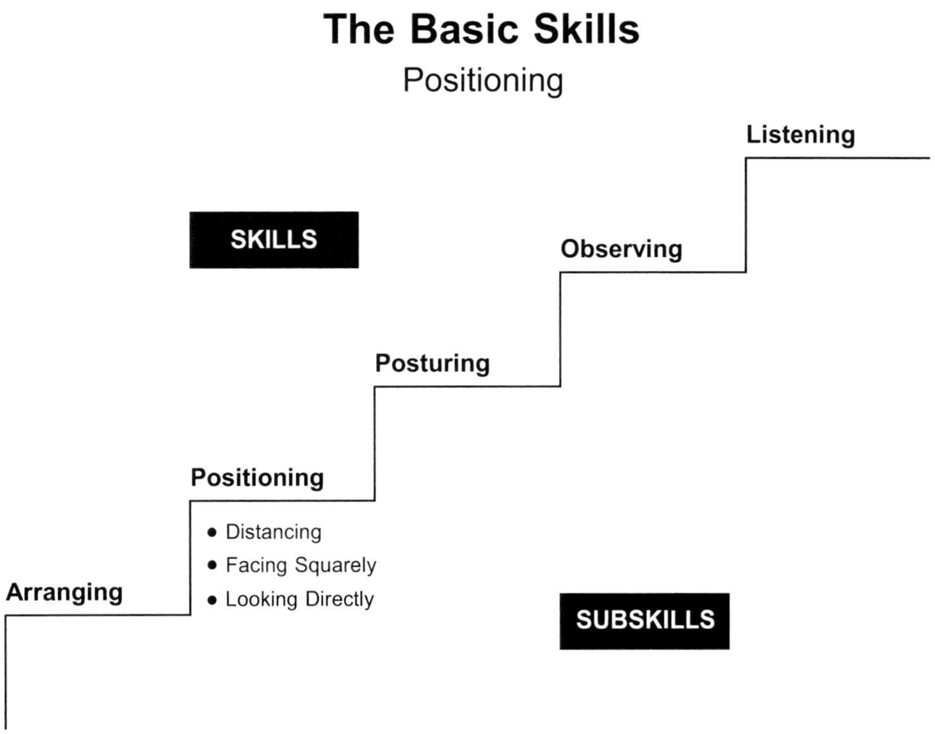

The Sub-skills of Positioning

Distancing. The first sub-skill of positioning is distancing. One of the obvious functions of establishing the appropriate *distance* from someone is to enable you to see and hear clearly. When your goal is communication, positioning yourself somewhere between 18 inches and 3 feet works best. If you are too close, you will risk threatening persons and you will break that "invisible zone" we all have around us. If you distance yourself more than 3 feet away, people may develop concern about your genuine interest in them.

It is very important to note that the appropriate distance between persons is specific to each culture and may vary with gender. Some cultures value closer proximity, while others view physical closeness as rude or threatening behavior. You must consider the cultural and gender influences involved in your interactions in order to employ these training skills and sub-skills more effectively. It is important to keep cultural and gender differences in mind in your daily interactions.

If for any reason you anticipate trouble with someone who could possibly injure you, give yourself extra distance. Those who work in criminal justice settings typically allow 3½ feet as a norm so that they have time to react to danger. It is important for section managers to be aware that distance may nonverbally send positive and negative messages. Such awareness will provide a good start to your communication efforts.

Exercise 5: Distancing

Describe an instance when the distance between you and a person or group made communication difficult for you.

_____

_____

_____

Why? _____

_____

Describe an instance when the distance between you and a person or group made communication comfortable for you.

_____

_____

_____

Why? _____

_____

Facing squarely. The second sub-skill of positioning is facing squarely. When you squarely face almost anything you do, you can perform better. This is also true in your communication efforts. *Facing squarely* allows you to use the least effort to see the important nonverbal clues and keeps you from being distracted by other activities in the immediate area. Facing someone squarely also sends the non-verbal message that he/she has your complete, undivided attention and that you are truly listening to him/her. This puts the person in a more comfortable position and facilitates a more open interaction. Being squared is an important communication and management skill.

Exercise 6: Facing Squarely

Describe a time when either you or someone else did not squarely face you during an encounter and the impact that had on the interaction.

_____

_____

_____

_____

_____

Looking directly. The third sub-skill of positioning is *looking directly.* How many times have you heard or said that you could tell someone was not being honest because he/she wouldn't look you or someone else in the eye? Not that there's much validity to this test, but it seems to be used often. The reason for mentioning the statement is that people really believe that important messages are communicated by facial expressions and the eyes—and they are!

Please note that what particular message is conveyed is culturally dependent. In many cultures, persons who look you in the eye seem more interested, intense, concerned, etc. However, in other cultures, direct eye contact is viewed as aggressive and offensive. You may infer anxiety in shifting eyes and fatigue. Smiles, frowns, and perspiration can also lead to several important inferences. You can see why looking directly is an essential part of good positioning and why it is important to remain aware of cultural diversity when practicing this sub-skill.

In many cultures, people who look you in the eye seem more interested, intense, concerned, etc. However, in other cultures, direct eye contact is viewed as aggressive and offensive.

Exercise 7: Looking Directly

When you look directly at someone, what are the things that you believe provide you with reliable information?

smile = good mood, more agreeable to a conversation

frown/finger pointing/carotid artery = negative mood or emotional state, possibly anxious, less agreeable to a conversation, possible conflict situation

Describe an instance when eye contact with someone else made you uncomfortable.

- When it was culturally unacceptable
- When the person was paranoid or distrusting
- When the person was mentally ill
- When the person was embarrassed
- When the person was angry (e.g., road rage)

Posturing

The third skill of the Basic Skills Set is *posturing*. It takes energy to have good posture. One of the clearest signals of being tired or having low energy is poor body posture. When you stand or sit upright, it communicates your preparedness to function. People sense your interest and your confidence by your posture. Good posture assists you in sizing up situations. The sub-skills of posturing are listed in Figure 5.

Figure 5. The Basic Skills: Posturing

The Basic Skills
Posturing

SKILLS

Listening

Observing

Posturing

- Erect Posture
- Forward Lean
- Eliminating Distracting Behaviors

Positioning

Arranging

SUBSKILLS

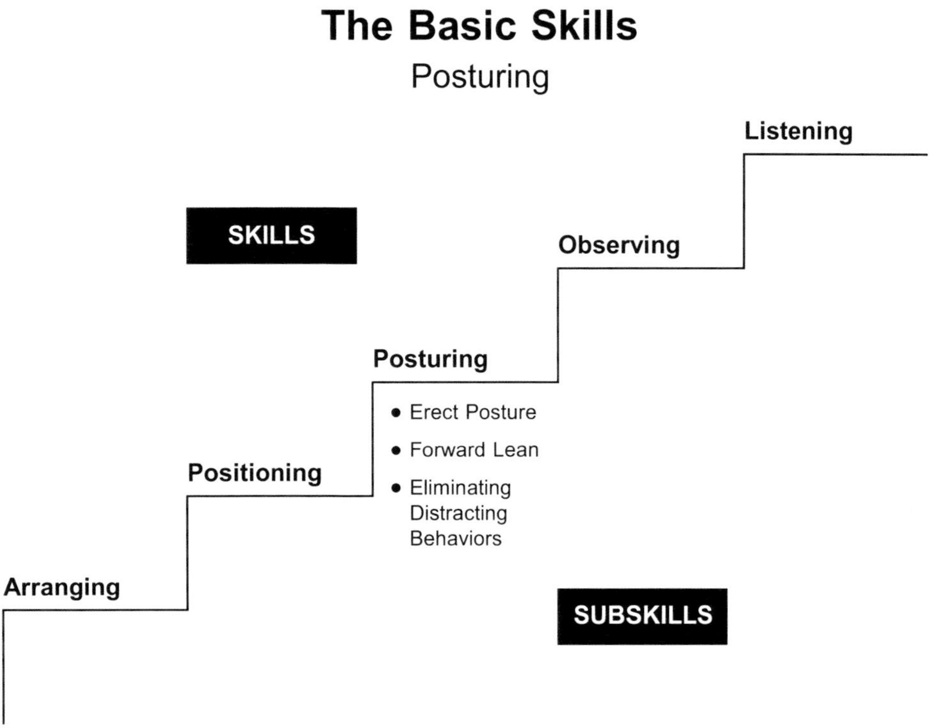

The Sub-Skills of Posturing

Erect posture: Standing and sitting. The first sub-skill of posturing is *standing and sitting erect*. If you appear not to be sitting or standing erect and you are in a sensitive situation where you want to control the conditions, you should sit and stand erect. It communicates a positive message. You are in control, you are ready, you care.

Because we are focusing on skills, it will be very appropriate for you to provide participant feedback on the impressions made. This does not mean you are judging each other as people. It means you are receiving feedback based on a model. It is up to you to decide whether or not the feedback is useful.

Forward lean. The second sub-skill of posturing is *inclining forward* slightly. If you want to appear in control, if you want to appear as if you know what you are doing, but not like you have to have your way, you should incline forward slightly. It shows interest or an inclination to help.

Eliminating distracting behaviors. The third sub-skill of posturing is *eliminating distractive behaviors.* If you lose control as a result of some "harmless" gestures, it isn't harmless. It may threaten someone who may not tell you. This may result in your losing control over a situation where you should have maintained control, cost you business, or damage a relationship.

Using the previous rationales, we will encourage you to give each other feedback about behaviors that may be distractive. You decide if you should work to eliminate them.

Exercise 8: Distracting Behaviors

List some distracting behaviors that you've experienced in others.

_____

_____

_____

_____

_____

List some distracting behaviors you've experienced in yourself (either *you* noticed them or *others* have told you about them).

_____

_____

_____

_____

_____

Practical Application Exercise

Here are the skills you have learned so far.

The Basic Skills
Sizing Up the Situation

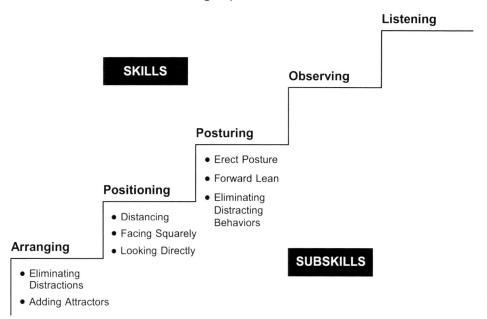

The instructor will guide you through several role plays so that you can practice these skills.

Sender	Receiver	Observers
Make a 60-second bio-sketch statement.	**Position:** Keep distance 3 to 5 feet. Face squarely. Maintain eye contact. **Posture:** Sit erect Lean slightly forward. Eliminate distracting behaviors.	Observe the listener's Distancing Facing squarely Looking directly Forward lean behaviors Provide feedback.

SENDERS: Do not provide expressions/statements that reveal personal content that might be embarrassing, intimate, or potentially harmful to yourself or others.

Observing

In the 1960s, William Condon began filming the interactions of couples and families in order to study the behaviors that each person manifested during a conversation. Each person in the conversation had a camera focused specifically on them.

In one sample, Condon filmed a 4.5 second interaction between a man, woman, and child over dinner. The woman says, "You all should come around every night. We never had a dinner time like this in months."

Condon then broke the film down into individual frames of 1/45th of a second each. What he discovered was a kind of social dance occurring between all of the participants. Each person, within the space of two or three individual frames (that's 3/45th of a second), would move something—a shoulder, cheek muscle, eyebrow, hand, etc.—then sustain it, stop it, change directions, and start again. He called these "micro movements." And the micro movements revealed a Social Synchrony. These rhythmic shifts of body and face were in harmony among three people. (e.g., the wife turning her head exactly as the husband's hands come up).

Condon called the phenomenon Interactional Synchrony. Subsequent research has shown that, besides gesturing and conversational rhythm (i.e., paralanguage), the voice volume and pitch also came into balance (i.e., speech rate equalizes).

Observing is the fourth skill of the Basic Skills Set. *Observing* means making inferences about what we see. Appearances, behavior, and environment are the things from which we make inferences (an inference is a conclusion or deduction). Clear observations and accurate inferences enable you to understand. Understanding (empathy) is the key to successful management and relationships. Because much reliable communication is nonverbal, we can learn about others' feelings and messages when we learn to observe and make accurate inferences. Figure 6 lists the sub-skills of observing.

Figure 6. The Basic Skills: Observing

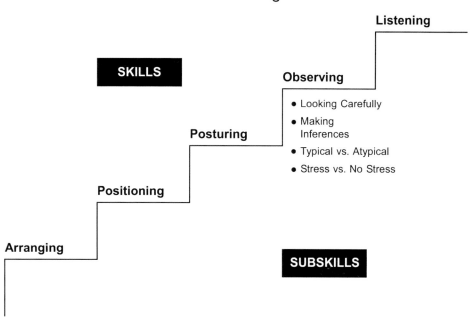

The Basic Skills
Observing

The Sub-Skills of Observing

Looking carefully. The first sub-skill of observing is *looking carefully*. Most of us believe that we see what is really going on around us. However, research suggests otherwise. In studies involving eyewitness accounts of staged robberies, witnesses who watched the same video reported variances in the number of suspects, what the robbers were wearing, and what type of getaway car was used. These studies point out that although we *think* we see what is happening, we miss a great deal. Therefore, we must make a concerted effort to let go of what we think we see, and truly look carefully and with an open mind.

The question is, for what are you looking?

- **Appearances:** Things you can observe.

  A display that could be observed even if a person was not behaving (even when dead!).

  Example: A person has no clothes on, or a person is a Caucasian male who is wearing a blue wool suit.

- **Behaviors:** Actions you can observe.

  What someone is doing that you can see.

  Example: A person is blinking their eyes rapidly.

- **Environment:** The context of the situation.

  Example: A person is with a group or is at a workstation.

Vision is the primary sense we use for observation. But there are some things you might not have known about our sight. For instance, did you know our eyes are our first step to listening? We blink every 2 to 10 seconds, which means your eyes are closed at least 30 minutes a day just from blinking. Pilots blink less often than co-pilots. Drivers blink less often in heavily congested traffic compared to lonely country roads. We blink more when we are angry or anxious or excited. Fatigue, alcohol, and drugs can make blinking less crisp.

Eye contact can sooth and calm another person.

Our eyes have to be trained to comprehend reality. Subliminal messaging acts on our visual sense. Volunteers sat in front of a computer displaying neutral faces. Unbeknownst to them, the computers subliminally flashed happy or angry faces for 1/25th of a second for very 1 second of neutral expression. Those volunteers who indicated they were thirsty before the experiment drank more than double after happy faces than after angry faces. Very thirsty volunteers were willing to pay up to three times more for a drink after "seeing" happy faces compared to angry faces. Subjects who were not thirsty prior to the experiment were unaffected. Newborn babies see the world upside down. It takes some time before the baby's brain learns to turn the picture right-side-up.

Individuals suffering from blindness as a result of non-eye disease (such as stroke) or traumatic brain injury sometimes experience "blindsight," or the ability to precisely locate or name objects placed in the blind visual field. These individuals invariably remind the researcher that they are blind and cannot see the object when asked to touch or name it, but when pressed, they are surprisingly precise and accurate. This suggests that the visual sense is working in that it is taking in the stimuli through the eye mechanism; however, the neural pathways in the brain that perpetrate the perception and image of the visual field are not working properly (Weiskrantz, 1995).

Making inferences. The second sub-skill of observing is making infer-ences. We naturally *make inferences* as a consequence of our observa-tions. Inferences allow us to understand and process what we see and hear.

We assess the clues from behavior, appearance, and environment and size up the meaning (make an inference). The standard you use for your inference may vary with the context from which and when you make your inference. Since inferences depend largely on your life experience for standard formulation, your inferences (conclusions) may be incorrect. Inferences are culturally, gendered, and experientially bound. That is why you should not act upon initial inferences unless you have no other reasonable choice. The more observations you make and the more you know about the context within which you make them, the more likely you are to be accurate. During this training, it will be very helpful if you reward your fellow classmates for accurate inferences. It will greatly increase everyone's skill in inference formulation.

Let's look at specific clues that deal with inferences about feelings, relationships, energy, and values. "Getting in touch with your feelings" is an expression widely used by many people. It seems to be common sense that behavior is often closely related to feelings. If you "feel" good, you generally "act" good. If you "feel" bad, efficiency is low and tolerance is limited. To manage effectively, it's useful to observe others or the clues that reveal the negative and positive aspects of another's feelings.

Making inferences about feelings. With increased observations, your judgment of others' feelings, or moods, can become sharper in determining the correct feeling category and intensity. This does not necessarily mean you must respond to a person's feelings, but recognizing them accurately will give you an interpersonal management advantage.

Exercise 9: Inferences about Feelings

What feeling word(s) would fit these examples?

Your co-worker is sitting at his desk staring straight ahead while drumming his or her pencil on the desk top:

Feeling word: _____

Inference: _____

Reason: _____

_____

_____

_____

Your supervisor storms into his/her office after attending a meeting with his/her manager and slams the door.

Feeling word: _____

Inference: _____

Reason: _____

_____

_____

_____

Making inferences about relationships. Besides being aware of the nonverbal cues that indicate the feelings of other people, you can further increase your effectiveness by looking for cues that indicate the nature of the relationship between you and others. The relationship between you and another person serves as a good indicator of future interaction. A person who has a positive relationship with you may be very helpful. A person who has a negative relationship with another may be a source of trouble.

In general, people can categorize relationships and feelings as positive, negative, or neutral. People who do things to make your job easier such as being cooperative or prompt, probably have, or want to have, a positive relationship with you. A person who tries to hassle you doesn't want to have a positive relationship with you. You need to know why.

The cues that help us make accurate inferences about relationships with others are also very important. Inferences about our relationships give us valuable information to help us understand and manage others.

Exercise 10: Inferences about Relationships

List two behaviors and/or appearances that indicate negative relationships.

1. _____

2. _____

What management problems might result from these behaviors and/or appearances?

_____

_____

_____

_____

List two behaviors and/or appearances that indicate positive relationships.

1. _____

2. _____

Making inferences about energy levels. We also make inferences about a person's energy levels.

Energy levels refer to a person's ability to act and maintain an action. This could refer to physical energy or psychic energy. Energy levels are typically measured, or observed, as high, moderate, or low.

Exercise 11: Inferences about Energy Levels

Describe two behaviors and/or appearances that reflect low energy.

1. _____

2. _____

What are the possible reasons for having low energy?

_____

_____

_____

_____

Describe two behaviors and/or appearances that reflect high energy.

1. _____

2. _____

What are the possible reasons for having high energy?

_____

_____

_____

_____

Why should you be concerned with whether a person has high or low energy?

_____

_____

_____

_____

Making inferences about values. Making accurate inferences about values tells you a lot about how persons prefer spending their energy. A good rule of thumb is "if you know how a person uses their energy, you know their values." Another way to look at is "if you know how a person spends their time, energy, and money, you know their values." Energy can be obviously measured in physical terms, but it can also be measured in money. Not only does understanding other persons' values aid in your understanding of them, but it also enables you to choose the most effective reinforcers to manage.

The reasons for your inferences should be based on visual cues from behaviors, appearances, and environment. Inferences stand the best chance of being accurate if they are based on detailed and concrete observations. Understanding the context (circumstances) surrounding your observations is also important. Being exposed to several detailed observations increases the reliability of your inferences.

Exercise 12: Inferences about Values

List three of your most important values:

1. _____

2. _____

3. _____

Deciding typical and atypical. The third sub-skill of observing is *deciding if things are typical or atypical*. The term "typical" describes a pattern of behavior that is common and would likely be associated with some element of healthy functioning. The term "atypical" describes a pattern of behavior that is uncommon and would likely be associated with some element of dysfunction. These terms may seem like unnecessary semantics to you, but it's important to understand that persons are at times not as they are typically. Managing and interacting with others will require your taking this into account.

Exercise 13: Typical/Atypical Behaviors

Describe your typical mood:

_____

_____

_____

_____

Describe your typical energy level:

_____

_____

_____

_____

Deciding stress or no stress. The fourth sub-skill of observing is _deciding if there is stress or no stress present_. Now that you have looked carefully, made inferences about feelings and energy level, and decided whether or not your observations reveal typical or atypical behavior, is it your conclusion that there is stress present? There are a couple of questions you can ask yourself that may help with your decision.

> **Question #1:** Would the indicators you have inferred from your observations mean stress is present for someone?

> **Question #2:** How does all you have observed impact you physically and emotionally (are there signals of stress being communicated to you by your body and mind)?

If you answer yes, then the probability is high that your observations have correctly inferred stress in the other person.

Exercise 14: Stress Inference

Describe how you know when you are stressed.

_____

_____

_____

_____

Practical Application Exercise

The Basic Skills
Sizing Up the Situation

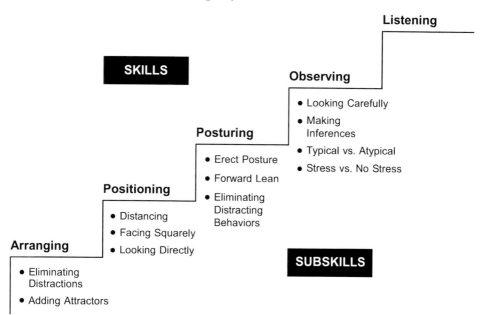

Sender	Receiver	Observers
Make a 60-second statement about a life experience.	Position Posture Observe: Describe speaker's appearance, behavior, environment. Infer speaker's feelings, relationships, energy levels.	Observe the receiver's Distancing Facing squarely Looking directly Forward lean Behaviors Record your own impressions of the speaker's feelings, relationships, energy levels, and values.

SENDERS: Do not provide expressions/statements that reveal personal content that might be embarrassing, intimate, or potentially harmful to yourself or others.

Listening

Listening is the fifth and final skill of the Basic Skills Set. This module could easily be entitled hearing because the only real evidence that listening has occurred is a response (behavior). Typically, the evidence is an active response from the listener that shows the content offered was actually "heard." An example would be a request that is acted upon— "It's awfully cold in the office," followed by someone adjusting the thermostat. Although nonverbal communication is considered, from a technical perspective, to make up most of the accurate message transacted, most people believe things would be much better if people would simply "listen" to them! See Figure 7.

Figure 7. The Basic Skills: Listening

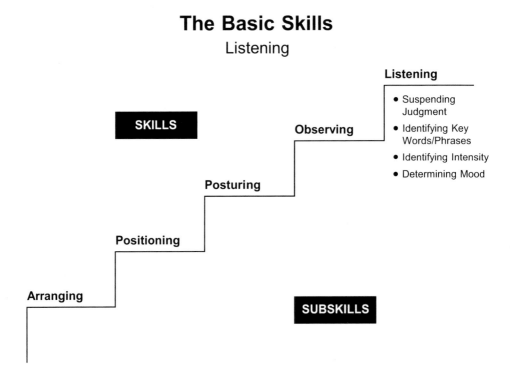

Preparation for good listening depends on your use of the Basic Skills. Arranging, positioning, posturing, and observing enhance hearing. Think of it as the preparation for the delivery of any skill. You must rehearse the Basics, or you will forever struggle. . . at anything!

Exercise 15: The Effective Listener

List below, in your own words, the characteristics that you value in a good *listener*.

_____

_____

_____

_____

_____

_____

List below, in your own words, the characteristics that you value in a good *communicator*.

_____

_____

_____

_____

_____

_____

The Sub-skills of Listening

Suspending judgment. The first sub-skill of listening is suspending judgment. Remember, the goal is to listen. Suspending judgment is critical if you are to achieve this goal. This doesn't mean you let someone "walk all over" you. It means understanding as much as possible. It doesn't mean agreeing in blanket fashion either. It means waiting until you have heard all the content before you respond. If after hearing the content you are compelled to offer your view, offer it. The other person will know, however, that you "have heard their story."

People who know they can tell their story to you fully, even when you may see the same situation differently, will respect you. Suspending judgment is not an easy thing to do because we live in a very competitive culture, and people are quick to judge even though they won't always let you know they have. When you don't immediately judge, you have set the ground rules and everyone can win.

It's important not to get confused about suspending judgment. Occasionally when involved in supervision or management, you must take into consideration existing company rules, violations, quality of work, etc. This is expected behavior. However, suspending judgment helps free people to tell more and to be more "up front." Remember, when you are in a position that requires judgment, *you are judging a person's actions—not the person*.

Why is suspending judgment important to listening?

- It allows you to *hear* what's being said.
- The speaker will *feel* heard.
- It *models* patience and respect.
- It *gains patience and respect* for you.

Identifying key words and phrases. The second sub-skill of listening is *identifying key words and phrases*. In different environments and context there are words and phrases that "stick out" or cause your adrenaline to race. These words and phrases are associated with recollections that have important meanings. At work, overhearing the word "downsize" may perk your ears to hear more. At home it may be "internal revenue" or "in-laws."

Listening is one of the universally valued skills of interpersonal communications. Being heard or understood is the real target. There are two tests to determine whether or not you have been listened to and heard. The first is a behavioral response. The listener proves hearing by doing something that is directly related to what has been said verbally or communicated nonverbally. For example, you ask a coworker to close your office door and the coworker closes the door.

The other is an utterance that contains the content, feelings, or both of the person who is speaking. Frequently persons believe they have been heard by others who nod or verbally respond with a generalized expression such as, "Uh-huh" or "Yes, I see." Neither, of course, contains any proof of being heard or understood. The skill of asking questions is taught in a later section. You will also learn the old journalism technique of the 5WH and how to find out whether your understanding of the answer was accurate.

Remember, these skills are useful in every interpersonal transaction. They are especially useful in management and supervisory circumstances. Once learned, you are in control of their use in any situation. If you need information, they are helpful. With practice, you will blend the skills into your repertoire so that they flow into your communications and become natural. You may experience awkwardness initially. You may also become somewhat frustrated with the formats your SoTelligence instructors use to guide you. As in any other effective training programs, when you begin experiencing results, you may insist you had these skills all the time and you just had not dusted them off until now.

A system that has been used effectively to identify key words and phrases in journalism, law enforcement, and education is the **5WH system.** The 5 Ws are *who, what, when, where,* and *why.* The H is *how.* Determining the answers to the 5WH should provide you with important information. The 5WH is easy to remember, and with a little practice combined with good interpersonal skill, you can become very effective at getting information you need.

Exercise 16: Identifying Key Words and Phrases

List two key words or phrases that would be important to you if you heard them in your **home** environment and why they would be important.

1. Word/Phrase: _____

_____

Reason for importance: _____

_____

_____

2. Word/Phrase: _____

_____

Reason for importance: _____

_____

_____

List two key words or phrases that would be important to you if you heard them in your **work** environment and why they would be important.

1. Word/Phrase: _____

_____

Reason for importance: _____

_____

_____

2. Word/Phrase: _____

_____

Reason for importance: _____

_____

_____

Identifying intensity. The third sub-skill of listening is *identifying intensity*. How intense an expression (verbal or nonverbal) is perceived is based on your subjective standards and the context in which it's experienced. Obviously stomping and screaming may be relatively ignored at a sporting event, but given the same expressions of intensity in the executive dining room or during a department meeting is quite another matter. As we become experienced and understand the context in which expressions are encountered, we learn how much energy to invest in particular situations.

During interpersonal interactions, there are guidelines we can use to help determine the significance any perceived intensity might have in our management. However, as with each of these skills, it is very important to maintain an awareness of cultural, gender, and other individual differences that result in varying interpretations of intensity.

Intensity involves an energy investment. When persons shout, they normally invest more energy than when they converse. We normally (or at least initially) are attentive to the decibels. Persons in distress shout. It doesn't mean that anyone but themselves can remove the stressor, but they initially want attention drawn to them. The same can be said of gestures. Persons expressing high intensity may signal their distress by waving their arms, shaking their heads and fists, etc.

Although we tend to think of intensity with relation to movement or increased decibels, when you establish a norm (what is typical) for a person or persons, quietness may reflect intensity. Some typically gregarious persons may be feeling and expressing intensity when they are very still and quiet. Remember it's the deviation from the norm that reflects intensity.

> As we become experienced and understand the context in which expressions are encountered, we learn how much energy to invest in particular situations.

Determining mood. The fourth sub-skill of listening is *determining the mood.* Moods act like filters. Mood is the feeling theme that we or others are experiencing. It is assessable by both observing and listening. A person's posture, gestures, and utterances help us infer and describe their mood. We may use many adjectives, but in general, mood is positive, negative, or neutral (or more simply good or bad). If we don't know a person, we use our own standards to assess mood. That's why it's so important to be honest with ourselves, so our standards are reliable when we use them as measures for other persons.

Practical Application Exercise

Suspending judgment, identifying the intensity, and determining the mood are sub-skills that are better practiced and learned from role-playing. During role-playing, we can observe all the nonverbal expressions and hear the volume, tone, and voice pitch.

Sender	Receiver	Observers
Make a 60-second statement about your vocational history.	Position Posture Observe Listen Suspend judgment... – Verbally – Nonverbally – Thoughts Identify key words/ phrases. State key words/ phrases. State a list of what was said.	Observe the receiver's Distancing Facing squarely Looking directly Forward lean Behaviors Identify: Key words/phrases Intensity of expression Mood Compare your observations with the listener's and provide feedback.

SENDERS: Do not provide expressions/statements that reveal personal content that might be embarrassing, intimate, or potentially harmful to yourself or others.

Basic Skills Set Summary

You have demonstrated the Basic Skills that are vital to your effectiveness as a skilled communicator. Arranging, positioning, posturing, observing, and listening, along with their sub-skills, are invaluable tools for all types of interpersonal interactions. Practice will allow you to use these skills freely and comfortably in your daily interactions. With continued use, you will be more efficient and less stressed.

The Basic Skills
Sizing Up the Situation

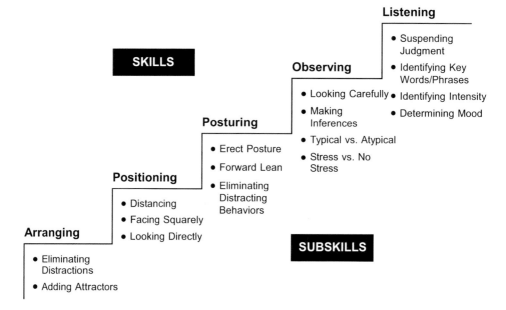

Listening
- Suspending Judgment
- Identifying Key Words/Phrases
- Identifying Intensity
- Determining Mood

Observing
- Looking Carefully
- Making Inferences
- Typical vs. Atypical
- Stress vs. No Stress

SKILLS

Posturing
- Erect Posture
- Forward Lean
- Eliminating Distracting Behaviors

Positioning
- Distancing
- Facing Squarely
- Looking Directly

Arranging
- Eliminating Distractions
- Adding Attractors

SUBSKILLS

Module 4: The Add-On Skills Set

Verbal Communication and Responding Techniques

Technique	Goal
Responding	Building rapport
Personalizing	Getting someone to take responsibility
Confronting	Opposing another person's thoughts, actions, emotions
Assertive	Stating your thoughts, actions, emotions
Self-disclosure	Telling someone something about yourself to build trust
Immediacy	Getting someone to focus on their present behavior
Probing	Drawing information from someone by asking relevant questions
Ability potential	Motivating someone who has lost confidence
Making requests	Asking someone to do something
Handling requests	Managing another person's request of you
Instruction	Telling someone "how" to do something
Information passing	Passing on information to someone else
Reinforcing	Using verbal and nonverbal behaviors to maintain desired behaviors

The Add-Ons: Responding

Whether your goal is to supervise, manage, lead, or simply build and maintain relationships, the Add-On Skills of responding and asking relevant questions is where the "rubber meets the road" (Figure 8). Learning to effectively use these skills can help you hurdle the obstacles you will face during challenging interpersonal transactions and interactions. Even if your goal is to just get along well enough to carry out primary responsibilities, these skills will help you maintain working *non-adversarial relationships*. If you want to build healthy, productive relationships, responding and asking relevant questions will enable you to do so.

If you need information from someone else, the Add-On Skills can help you get it without being forceful or intimidating. These skills can also help you insulate yourself from being manipulated.

Figure 8. The Add-On Skills: Communicating

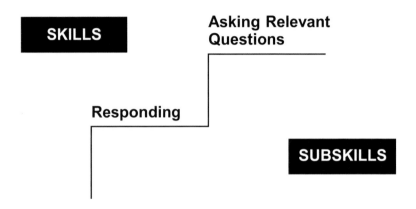

The Add-On Skills
Communicating

Responding

Responding involves the accurate paraphrasing of your understanding of what you have seen or heard. It offers proof to others that you have listened and observed. Each sub-skill of responding has its own components (Figure 9).

Figure 9. The Add-On Skills: Responding

The Add-On Skills
Responding

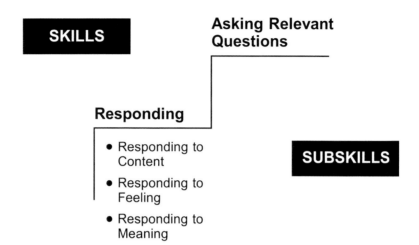

The Sub-Skills of Responding

Responding to content. The first sub-skill of responding is *responding to content*. Remember, this is a skill with which you supplement your Basic Skill Set. It is important that you suspend judgment while responding. If your goal is to get information, communicate, manage, build relationships, etc., being judgmental restricts you from attaining your goals. This doesn't mean you cannot express your opinion or enforce rules. It also does not mean that you allow people to abuse you or that you are forced to agree with them. It means that when you respond, you encourage people to talk more. It means you are interested, and it models the behavior that you value. You reflect on the key words and expressions you hear and see and paraphrase your summary to the person. See Figure 10.

Figure 10. The Add-On Skills: Responding to Content

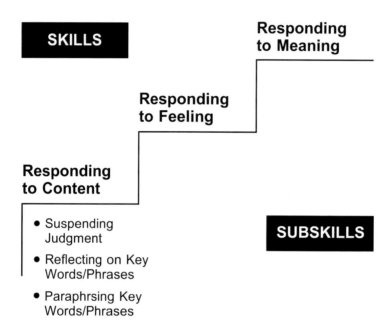

The Add-On Skills
Responding to Content

Suspending judgment. The first component of the sub-skill responding to content is *suspending judgment*. To hear what may be helpful or useful will be best achieved by keeping another person from "clamming up." To listen without judgment, even if only temporarily, is the best method to accomplish this end. It may not seem logical to suspend judgment when someone has obviously broken a rule or violated policy. But you must remember that it is recognized that you do not wish to reinforce irresponsibility. The goal initially, and perhaps only temporarily, is to keep or encourage open communication.

Reflecting on key words and phrases. The second component of the sub-skill responding to content is *reflecting on key words and phrases*. The 5WH system (who, what, when, where, why, and how) introduced previously is very useful as an intrapersonal skill. Asking these questions of yourself as you listen to content being expressed will allow you to implement this component. The key words and phrases are the answers to the 5WH questions posed intrapersonally.

Paraphrasing key words and phrases. The third component of the sub-skill responding to content is *paraphrasing key words and phrases*. Paraphrasing demonstrates that you have heard what the other person has said without judgment. Perhaps the best way to illustrate an example of paraphrasing is to provide an example. A person says: "I'll never learn to use this word processing program at the level they want me to. I might as well throw in the towel now." You apply the 5WH system. You select the key words and phrases, apply the third component of responding to content, and paraphrase your response to the statement. "You are not learning the word processing program as well as they want you to and are ready to quit."

It is suggested that you use formats when you are responding. Formats are like leads such as:

"You're saying_____." or

"What I hear you saying is_____." or

"You look _____."

Exercise 17: Responding to Content

Write an example of a response you might make to an observation you have made.

"You (it) look(s) _____

_____

_____

_____

_____

Write an example of a response you might make to something you have heard.

"You're saying _____

_____

_____

_____

_____

Practical Application Exercise

Your instructor will guide you through several role plays that will enhance your skills for responding to content.

The Add-On Skills
Responding to Content

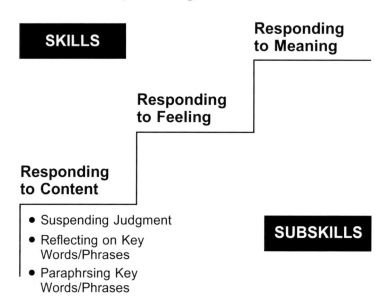

| SKILLS |
| Responding to Meaning |
| Responding to Feeling |
| Responding to Content |
- Suspending Judgment
- Reflecting on Key Words/Phrases
- Paraphrsing Key Words/Phrases

| SUBSKILLS |

Sender	Receiver	Observers

Role play 30 seconds.	Position
	Posture
	Observe
	Listen
	
	Pause and reflect (5WH).
		Observe the listener's
		  Positioning
		  Posturing
		  Observing
		  Listening skills and
		    behaviors

Provide feedback.	Paraphrase:
	  "You're saying..."
	  "You (it) look(s)..."
		Rate the listener's responses.
		
		Provide feedback.

SENDERS: Do not provide expressions/statements that reveal personal content that might be embarrassing, intimate, or potentially harmful to yourself or others.

Responding to feeling. The second sub-skill of responding is *responding to feeling*. It is the skill of expressing verbally, or nonverbally, the understanding that you have of the mood, emotion, or effect of persons. Responses to feeling may have several possible values. Persons may feel rewarded by you paying attention to their feelings thus encouraging them to tell you more about the causes of those feelings. If feelings are intense, talking about them may diffuse the intensity. See Figure 11.

Figure 11. The Add-On Skills: Responding to Feeling

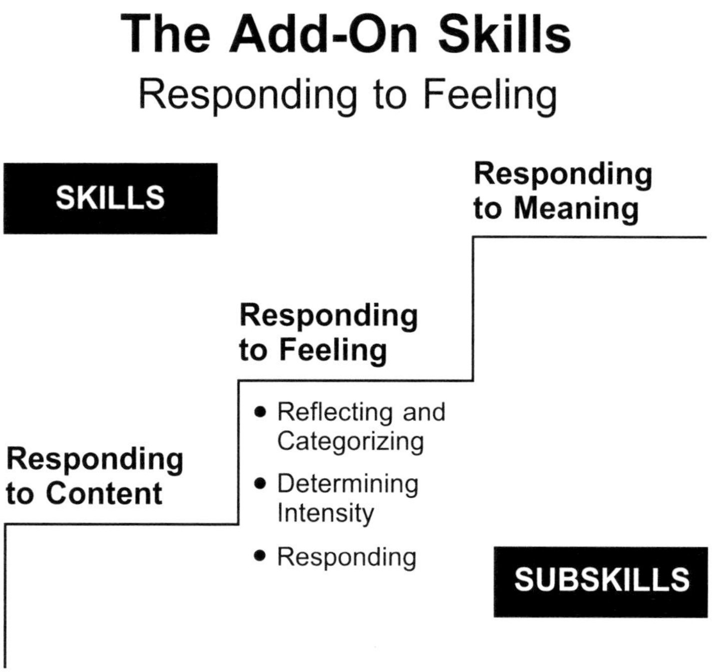

The Add-On Skills
Responding to Feeling

SKILLS

Responding to Meaning

Responding to Feeling

- Reflecting and Categorizing
- Determining Intensity
- Responding

Responding to Content

SUBSKILLS

Reflecting and categorizing. The first component of the sub-skill responding to feelings is *reflecting on the feeling and determining its category*. There are seven categories for your consideration that cover most of the feelings (emotions) people experience (happy, sad, angry, scared, confused, strong and weak). Based on what you see and hear and your life experiences, you can quickly get an understanding of not only the feeling but also its intensity. You will have an opportunity to assess your depth of understanding of each category later in the section.

Determining intensity. The second component of the sub-skill responding to feeling is *determining the intensity*. There will be times when you don't have a history with someone, so you will have to rely on your experience. You should ask yourself these questions: "When I behave like what I'm observing and hearing, how do I feel and how intense am I?" and "When I have experienced others behaving in that fashion in the past, how must they have felt and how intensely?"

Using a standard of high, moderate, and low is usually specific enough to accurately describe the intensity of one's feelings. A rough assessment of high intensity would be when a feeling deviates significantly from the norm you are using. Volume (high or low) and gestures are criteria that are helpful. High intensity would be a very loud (or very quiet) voice and accompanying gestures that would suggest significant deviation, like shouting and fist clenching. Low intensity would be a quiet but discernible voice and an absence of gestures. Moderate would be voice and gesture that may not cause notice in either direction. SoTelligence makes no claim of these standards being a science, but when you offer a rationale for your assessment, you'll probably be accurate. When you are in the skills activities, compare your intensity assessments with others, and you'll further refine your standards. Also, remember to be aware of cultural and gender norms and differences in interpreting intensity. They may make a difference. Do cultural and gender norms differences exist in your life? How are they significant or insignificant?

The Feeling Word Matrix on the following page gives you the opportunity to determine how many words you have in your vocabulary to describe emotions. There are no right or wrong answers for this exercise. It is simply an opportunity for you to examine what words (adjectives) you use to express intensity in each category and what others use as well. If consensus helps you fine-tune your feeling words, you should become more precise in your responses to feeling and increase your feeling word vocabulary. These categories are somewhat arbitrary. There is no definitive science from which to draw for better direction. Experience shows that feelings are the result of something, and negative feelings may cause us to function less well than we, and those around us, would like.

Feeling Word Matrix

Category	High Intensity	Moderate Intensity	Low Intensity
Happy			
Sad			
Scared			
Angry			
Confused			
Strong			
Weak			

Responding. The third component of the sub-skill responding to feeling is *responding* using the most appropriate category level of intensity. In situations in which you want to remain in control, you want to respond with an intensity that is as equal to that of the other person. When you respond with a lower level of intensity, you may have a calming effect that can help diffuse a volatile situation. A response with the same or greater level of intensity (if the emotion is negative) may escalate the situation, sending it out of anyone's control. Responding with the proper level of intensity is an effective management tool.

We are not taught, as Americans, to develop a vocabulary for our emotions. It's socially and culturally OK for us to talk about being happy or mad and sometimes being sad or strong, but we tend to *not* talk about being confused or weak—that would reveal our vulnerability. Who do you think tends to do better on this, men or women? Women—in our culture they are the emotion "carriers"—they are encouraged from infancy to display and *recognize* emotions, and that is reinforced through our relationships, advertisements, and our values. Males are taught to be instrumental in their value systems (i.e., objective, reality-bound, etc.). Consider the British Widower's study. In the late 1950s, 4,486 widowers aged 55 years and older were followed for nine years since the death of their wives in 1957. Of these 213 died during the first six months of bereavement, 40% above the expected rate for married men of the same age. After the initial six months, the mortality rate fell gradually to that of married men (Parkes & Brown, 1969). Developing a vocabulary for feelings is critical if we are to be able to accurately recognize emotions in others as well as in ourselves. The vocabulary gives voice to our internal states allowing us the opportunity to diffuse those emotions rather than keep them pent up and subject to the power of an emotional pressure cooker.

Emotional Intelligence

The *eloquent lover* may lack passion;
but the *inarticulate hater*
poses a far greater danger
than the *vituperative* one.

Alexithymia
A (lexi) (thymia)
Non lexical (language) sensations.
No words for feelings.

We have words for objects, people, ideas, and experiences We even instinctively understand utterances that reflect emotions such as whimpers, shrieks, sighs, and coos. But most of us have very few words for our emotions.

Exercise 18: Practical Application

Your instructor will guide you through several role plays that will enhance your responding to content and feeling skills.

The Add-On Skills
Responding to Feeling

SKILLS

Responding to Meaning

Responding to Feeling

- Reflecting and Categorizing
- Determining Intensity
- Responding

Responding to Content

- Suspending Judgment
- Reflecting on Key Words/Phrases
- Paraphrsing Key Words/Phrases

SUBSKILLS

Sender	Receiver	Observers

Make a 20 to 30 second statement of something that emotionally affects you.
 	
Repeat above.
 	
Provide feedback.
	Position
	Posture
	Observe
	Listen
	Pause and reflect (5WH)
	
	Respond to content: "You're saying _____."
	
	Respond to feeling: "You feel _____."
		Observe the receiver's
		  Positioning
		  Posturing
		  Observing
		  Listening skills and
		    behaviors
		
		Write your own responses.
		
		Rate the receiver's responses.
		
		Provide feedback.

SENDERS: Do not provide expressions/statements that reveal personal content that might be embarrassing, intimate, or potentially harmful to yourself or others.

Responding to meaning. The third sub-skill of responding is *responding to meaning.* This skill combines feelings with content, which we call meaning. Feelings are not created in a vacuum. Instead, they are caused by the content of circumstances. Content sometimes has implications to itthat, with more understanding, gives much sharper and broader meaning. For example, "You feel bad because you lost the game," does not provide as clear a picture as, "You feel bad because you lost the game and you believe it was your fault or you let the team down."

The more you can see or experience something the way the other person is experiencing it, the more meaning you can give the content in your response. Exposing the feelings and meanings can lead to resolving discrepancies (Figure 12).

Figure 12. The Add-On Skills: Responding to Meaning

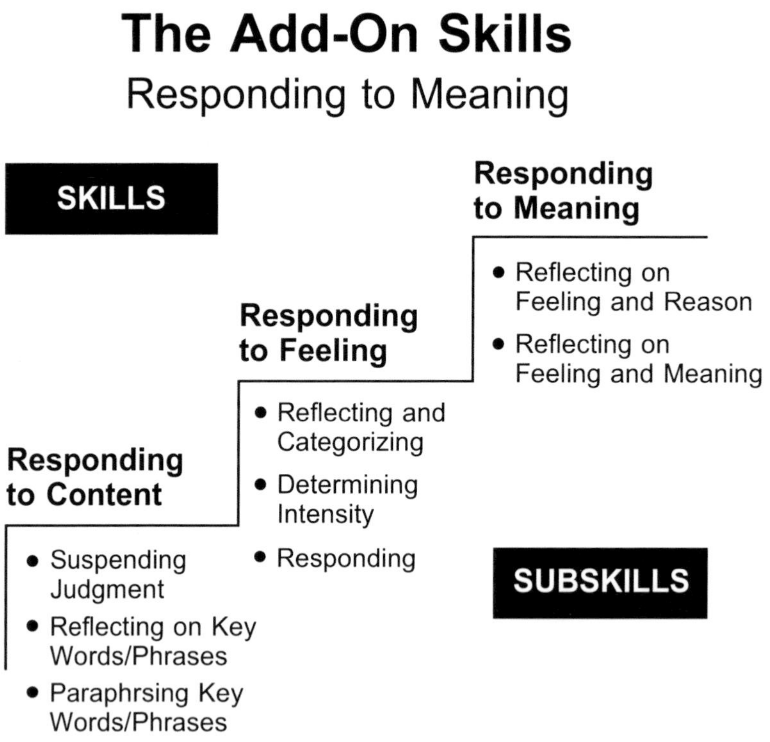

The Add-On Skills
Responding to Meaning

SKILLS

Responding to Meaning
- Reflecting on Feeling and Reason
- Reflecting on Feeling and Meaning

Responding to Feeling
- Reflecting and Categorizing
- Determining Intensity
- Responding

Responding to Content
- Suspending Judgment
- Reflecting on Key Words/Phrases
- Paraphrsing Key Words/Phrases

SUBSKILLS

Reflecting on feeling and reason/reflecting on feeling and meaning. The first component of the sub-skill responding to feeling and meaning requires *reflecting on the feeling and the reason for the feeling.* The second component of the sub-skill responding to feeling and meaning requires a *response to both feeling and meaning.* Both components provide meaning.

Throughout your professional career and in your personal life, there have been many difficult interpersonal transactions that you have had to manage. As you are aware, in many of them you will not control the conditions to change things. What you do have, or can have with these skills, is the ability to minimize the stress that can result. Similar to damage control, you can manage the stress that may evolve and keep it to a minimum. Research has proven this is possible if you are skilled in these components.

We also know that without skill, you may make matters worse, raise intensity, say provocative things, and in general lose ground rather than gain it. An example of this is when you listen to another person who doesn't have the facts as you have them. Losing control of your feelings will not likely get the facts straight.

If you are not the policy maker, you probably can't force someone to behave or respond differently if their facts are not accurate. Your highest probability of stress control in these situations is to be responsive and give your version of the situation. Bottom line—don't let your emotions rule the situation. If it's a management problem in a work place, you, of course, need to follow the established procedures after you have managed using all your interpersonal skill. At least you have managed yourself and set a *model* of behavior for managing differences.

Remember we are not asking you to give yourself up when you have a right to "stay the course." The next time someone blames you for something and directs their negative feelings toward you, respond (not agree) to them before you do anything else. Experience shows that by being decent, you achieve more control.

Bottom line:
Don't let your emotions rule the situation.

Exercise 19: Managing Differences by Responding

Write a response you may make to the example provided.

"You just never do your part. You wait and wait, and then after I've nearly finished it, you ask if you can help."

Content: _____

_____

Intensity: _____   Feeling word: _____

Reason: _____

_____

Your full response: _____

_____

_____

Exercise 20: Managing Real Life by Responding

Describe a short scenario (a life drama or scene) that was difficult for you and your response/reaction to that scenario. Using the formats previously described as a guide, write a brief response to the feeling and meaning that you believe would demonstrate an improvement over the way you responded before.

Scenario:

_____

_____

_____

_____

How you responded before and the outcome it produced:

_____

_____

_____

_____

Your response now:

_____

_____

_____

_____

_____

> **Remember, it's the deviation from the norm that reflects intensity.**

The Mathematics of Divorce

– John Gottman –

The Specific Affect Coping System (SPAFF)

John Gottman received a psychology degree after extensive training at MIT in mathematics. He became intrigued with the idea that mathematical processes could be applied to human behavior. Beginning in the 1980s, he began taping couples as they talked about non-contentious things (where to go on vacation, what to eat for dinner, etc.). Each person is filmed separately while they talk to each other for 15 minutes. Each person's facial expressions and tone of voice are coded (1 per second; 15 minutes yields 900 codes for each person).

There are 20 separate codes for emotions:

Positive	Neutral	Negative
Joy (+4)	Neutral	Contempt (−4)
Humor (+4)	Tension	Disgust (−3)
Affection (+4)		Defensive (−2)
Validation (+4)		Belligerent (−2)
Interest (+2)		Stonewalling (−2)
		Domineering (−1)
		Anger (−1)
		Whining (−1)
		Sadness (−1)

With more than 3,000 couples in the database, Gottman can predict divorce within 15 years with 90% accuracy if he analyzes only 15 minutes of film. If he analyzes for 1 hour, he can predict divorce within 15 years with 95% accuracy.

A significant finding: the higher the percentage of expressed *disgust* and *contempt,* the higher the likelihood of divorce.

Social Intelligence Skills

Emotional Intensity

On Killing, Dave Grossman

- Our optimal state of arousal is between 115–145 heartbeats per minute (aka, "the zone").

- Above 145 beats, complex motor skills start to break down.

- At 175 beats, mental processing breaks down. The neocortex stops processing, and the reptilian cortex (i.e., midbrain) takes over.
  - Vision becomes restricted.
  - Behavior becomes inappropriately aggressive.
  - Blood is withdrawn from our outer muscle layer into the core muscles, establishing our "body armor."
  - Bowel and bladder control is often lost.

To avoid the consequences of over arousal, you must continuously rehearse actions, thoughts, and emotions (skills) that will help you control the perceived threat.

The more you repeat a positive behavior and allow your senses and the neocortex to work together, the less you will be influenced by the reptilian brain, allowing you to *think* clearly and *act* skillfully.

Destructive Social Behaviors

We're going to take a moment to talk about destructive social behaviors, and we are inserting this here in the "emotions" section because most destructive behaviors are considered destructive because of the passionate and heightened emotional responses they often seek and find. Most of these behaviors involve our verbal actions, again stressing the importance that we *choose* our responses wisely. So, here we review some of the research around *profanity, gossip, rudeness, jealousy,* and *showing contempt and disgust.* Of course, this is not a complete list of destructive social behaviors, but the topics have been chosen with a purpose. These represent the types of behaviors that seem to "slip in" to our daily interactions with friends, family, and co-workers. Unlike overt bullying; social, emotional, and mental abuse; and other types of hostile actions, these are the kinds of behaviors that often begin as a private joke or teasing and escalate over time in both frequency and intensity until they are embedded in our relationships and in our communication paths.

Remember, context is key. Behaviors in one setting do not necessarily translate to another setting and/or a different group of interactants. For example, studies of team cohesion among athletes indicate that some behaviors (i.e., inequity among team members, embarrassment, and ridicule) deter cohesion while other behaviors (i.e., bragging, sarcasm, and teasing) promote team cohesion (Turman, 2003). However, these same behaviors in a different setting might result in different perceptions and outcomes.

Profanity (also Cussing, Swearing, Cursing)

Like many social behaviors, the use of profanity must be considered in the context of the era. But regardless of the time frame, the use of profanity elicits physical effects ranging from the elevated cardiac rates, increased Galvanic skin responses, blushing, trembling, shallow breathing, and—in extreme cases—the loss of bodily functions such as bowel and bladder control (LaPointe, 2006).

According to the *Oxford English Dictionary,* cussing is language that is lacking in refinement, good taste, uncultured, or ill-bred (i.e., primitive). There are three categories of profanity:

- Sexual
- Religious (or Deity)
- Excretory

In the 1970s, rates of profanity were measured at an average of 7.75% of individuals' vocabularies (Nerbonne and Hipskind, 1972). Children were found to use profanity not only to gain attention but also to express frustration or anger, provoke adults, disrupt activities, imitate peers, or simply as a form of expression (Bloom, 1977). Among undergraduates, arguments containing profanity were no more persuasive than arguments devoid of profanity. In fact, profanity in communication lowered the perceived credibility of the speaker—especially if the speaker was a woman (Bostrom et al., 1973). Counselors/therapists who used profanity were experienced as less effective and satisfying (Heubusch, 1977). However, cultural context influenced these findings. Among African-American young adults, profanity was described as a method for controlling anger during a game called "The Dozens" that involved two players uttering profanity about each other's family members (Savage and Tapley, 1976).

In the 1980s, replication studies of profanity and counselors/therapists indicated that physical attractiveness influenced the perception of effectiveness of counselors/therapists who used profanity. Paradise et al. (1980) found that the use of profanity, regardless of the physical attractiveness of the counselor/therapist, resulted in less favorable ratings for the counselor/therapist. When profanity was present, women were rated more positively than men. And, physically attractive counselors/therapists were judged to have more favorable attributes, regardless of their use of profanity. Undergraduates judging cartoons with absent, mild, or strong profane captions revealed that when profanity was absent, there was no difference between men and women in the "funniness" rating of the cartoon. However, when there was mild or strong profanity present, men found the cartoons significantly funnier compared to women's evaluations (Sewell, 1984). Self-assessments of profanity indicated that female undergraduates used profanity significantly less often than males, and the women felt that the use of profanity was inappropriate more often compared to men (Selnow, 1985).

Research on profanity in the 1990s revolved around the areas of compliance and neurophysiological functions. Kurklen and Kassinove (1991) and Sazar and Kassinove (1991) replicated research that found that the use of profanity reduced compliance with requests. [Zencius et al. (1990)] discovered that the use of immediate feedback in therapeutic settings with a brain-injured young male actually reduced the amount of profanity the male used in occupational therapy sessions, speech therapy sessions, and in social situations.

In 1969, Cameron found that every 14th word out of 67,000 words was profanity—that's 4 to 13% of our everyday speech. In the current decade, much of the research on profanity has centered on the use of profanity on television. In 2001, an analysis of shows aired on seven broadcast networks (including ABC, CBS, FOX, and NBC) between 8:00 p.m. and 11:00 p.m. revealed an average of 958 incidents of offensive language—evenly spread between the "children's" hour of 8:00 p.m.– 11:00 p.m. and the "adult" hour of 10:00 p.m.–11:00 p.m. (Kaye and Sapolsky, 2004). This is almost double the average amount of profanity used on the same networks throughout the 1990s. Although only inferences can be made, the contribution of television to the increases in the use of profanity among young children and adolescents seems to be strongly indicated.

Our motivations to cuss might be:

- Psychological: Release emotional tension
- Social: Draw attention to self
- Linguistic: Out of habit
- Power: Assert a position
- Informality: Break down social boundaries

Although cussing among women is on the rise, it is still a stereotypically male trait. The relationship between the participants affects the presence and amount of cussing. Intimate and less formal groups are more likely to experience cussing—especially if the topic is casual or impassioned. If there is a wide power distance among group members, cussing is less likely by the lower-ranking group members, but more likely among the upper-ranked members. People of all ages and ranks are less likely to cuss when they are in a positive mood. However, married women with children reported higher frequency than single women with children.

Cussing is perceived differently based on who is doing the cussing, where the cussing is being performed, and why the cussing is occurring. Cussing is often thought of as a group identity or affiliation strategy ("cusses like a sailor"). In the United States, cussing is regarded as a masculine activity (until recently). Men swear twice as frequently as women and use different swear words. Feminist women reported a higher use than did non-feminist women. Fathers are more likely to swear in front of children than mothers. People who swore were rated lower in their socio-intellectual status compared to people who refrained from cussing. People who swear less are more attractive and desirable to work with.

Swearing while alone vs. at another person vs. about other people not present affected people's perceptions of its negativity. When there was no perceived justification, cussing was judged as highly offensive. Ninety percent of women surveyed found it to be aversive in a public setting.

Sexual profanity is rated as the most offensive and indicates less social control; however, the force behind the word really determines its negativity.

Gossip (Chit Chat, Idle Talk, Girl Talk, Shooting the Breeze, Killing Time)

"Rumor is used to explain, justify, and provide meaning for emotional interests associated with issues of importance (Pendleton, 1998; Rosnow, 2001), gossip consists of talk about people for the purpose of exchanging information, entertainment, gaining influence or social control (Krumm, 2001)" (as cited in [Houmanfar and Johnson, 2003]; Guerin and Miyazaki, 2006). Foster (2004) attempts to operationalize the term further by stating that it is typically about a third party not present, involves evaluative content (both positive and negative), is attenuated by specific situational factors (such as timing and setting), and serves social functions such as facilitating information exchange, providing recreation and entertainment, providing an outlet for hostility, creating group solidarity, teaching group norms, determining guilt or innocence, and enabling memory construction for larger numbers of individuals in our group.

Wert and Salovey (2004) proposed that gossip helps us stay socially connected and interactive with others. Often, it is the only source for social information. They also contend that the negativity of gossip is often triggered by some event that induces us to compare ourselves with another person in terms of our social identity, self-evaluation, self-improvement, and self-enhancement.

Baumeister et al. (2004) asserts that gossip is simply an extension of observational learning, as gossip generally conveys the rules for appropriate behavior in a group, the consequences for disobeying the rules, and the rewards for following the rules. From this perspective, it is easier to understand why gossip may involve both positive comments and strangers.

In an effort to understand the transmission of gossip, Mesoudi et al. (2006) found that when gossip was defined as "information about intense third-party social relationships," it was transmitted more accurately and more frequently than information that did not contain social interaction information. Additionally, "everyday" social interactions were transmitted at the same frequency and accuracy rates as "intense" social interactions.

Investigations into Internet, e-mail, and texting technologies indicate that people are generally less inhibited about the messages they send/forward that contain unsubstantiated or gossip information, and this information is more often considered "truthful" and "trustworthy" by recipients. With an increased ability to reach large numbers of people in short periods of time, the Internet has become "a rapid and effective distribution mechanism for gossip, rumor, and urban legends" (Kibby, 2005).

A group of undergraduates were presented with gossip-like vignettes and then asked to recall what they had heard. Cues of attractiveness were recalled more often for female characters, and cues for wealth and status were recalled more often for male characters. Males recalled the events and descriptions of the male characters more saliently, and women recalled the events and descriptions of the female characters more saliently (DeBacker et al., 2007).

Another group of college students who were asked to rate 12 vignettes revealed that damaging and negative news about rivals along with positive news about friends and family was more likely to be passed along and more highly valued. Males were more interested in information about the male characters, and females were more interesting in information about the females. Males were more likely to gossip with their romantic partner, and girls were equally likely to gossip with their romantic partners as well as their girlfriends (McAndrew et al., 2007).

Children as young as seven understand that gossip can contribute to a person's reputation (Hill and Pillow, 2006).

Sarcasm

As early as the 1960s, sarcasm research revealed the positive and negative effects of sarcasm, or "wit." In 1965, Smith and White conducted research with Air Force airmen and found that individuals who were considered "witty" were considered less defensive and creative, especially in the area of problem-solving, but they were not necessarily considered effective leaders.

Individuals who tend to be good at detecting and understanding sarcasm also tend to be good at identifying the emotions in facial expressions (Simone Shamay-Tsoory as quoted in Svoboda, 2007). They also tend to possess more aggressive personalities (Albert Katz as quoted in Svoboda, 2007).

Children 5- to 10-years-old have difficulty interpreting sarcasm correctly. They either experience the sarcasm as deception because they don't understand that the speaker intentionally means something different from what he/she is saying, or they experience it as an error because they compare what the speaker is saying to their own knowledge, and they simply discard what they perceive to be an incorrect statement. Either of these conditions results in poor memory construction due to the child's inability to accurately comprehend sarcastic statements (Winner et al., 1987).

Individuals with damage to the right hemisphere of the brain have difficulty interpreting information about a speaker's emotional state, intentions, and beliefs, especially when the speaker uses sarcasm. Individuals with traumatic brain injury to the frontal lobe interpret the contradictory statements of sarcasm as relatively straightforward, but they have difficulty understanding the speaker's intent (McDonald, 2000; Shamay-Tsoory et al., 2007).

Some suggested rules for using sarcasm:
- Know your audience.
- Be alert to the tone of your written communications, like e-mail and texting.
- Examine your motivations. Are you really saying it to be funny or are you harboring some other feeling like anger.
- Err on the side of caution. If you aren't absolutely sure how it will be perceived, don't use it (Svoboda, 2007).

Rudeness

Undergraduates who have been primed to the concept of rudeness interrupted an authority figure conducting an experiment quicker and with more directness compared to undergraduates who had been primed to the concept of politeness (Bargh et al., 1996).

Studies on interruptions in dyadic conversations indicate that people who interrupt are judged to be "more indifferent, irrational, strong, argumentative, assertive, rude, dominant, competitive, overbearing, and concerned with self compared to persons who are interrupted" (LaFrance, 1992). Women who interrupt men are typically perceived as more rude, more irritable, and more concerned with themselves when compared to men who interrupt women or men who interrupt other men. In fact, these types of interruptions receive the most negative ratings and are often characterized as "an assault on the established power relations." Female observers of these conversations tend to judge the person who has been interrupted as more irritable compared to male judges.

Rudeness, regardless of whether it comes from an authority, comes from a third party, or is imagined, reduces our performances on routine tasks as well as on creative tasks while also decreasing our willingness to help (Porath and Erez, 2007).

Johnson and Indvik (2001) characterize rudeness in the workplace as "a culture that celebrates impulse over restraint, notoriety over achievement, rule-breaking over rule-keeping, and incendiary expression over minimal civility." Examples of rudeness in the workplace include the following:

- Condescending and demeaning comments
- Overruling decisions without offering a reason
- Disrupting meetings
- Giving public reprimands
- Talking about someone behind his/her back
- Giving others the silent treatment
- Ignoring people
- Not giving credit where credit is due
- Sexually harassing employees
- Giving dirty looks or negative eye contact
- Insulting and yelling at others

Anderson and Pearson (1999) surveyed employees who reported claims of incivility and found that

- 53% lost work time worrying about the incident or future interactions;
- 46% contemplated changing jobs to avoid the instigator;
- 37% believed their commitment to the organization declined;
- 28% lost work time avoiding the instigator;
- 22% decreased their work effort;
- 12% actually changed jobs to avoid the instigator; and
- 10% decreased the amount of time they spent at work.

Jealousy

Men tend to react jealously over the potential, or real, loss of a mate's physical infidelity (not emotional) while women tend to react jealously over the potential, or real, loss of a mate's emotional infidelity (Harris, 2003).

Among undergraduates, Dijkstra and Buunk (2002) found five characteristics in rivals that induced jealousy: Social Dominance, Physical Attractiveness, Seductive Behaviors, Physical Dominance, and Social Status. Heterosexual men reported more jealousy when the rival was high in Social Dominance, Physical Dominance, and Social Status. Heterosexual women reported more jealousy when the rival was high in Physical Attractiveness. Homosexual men reported higher levels of jealousy compared to homosexual women when the rival was high in Physical Dominance, and more jealousy compared to heterosexual men when the rival was high in Social Dominance. Homosexual women reported higher levels of jealousy compared to heterosexual women when the rival was high in Physical Attractiveness. In general, those who scored high in the Social Comparison Orientation assessment reported higher levels of jealousy, and this was especially true of women.

Jealousy is a major trigger for domestic violence. Puente and Cohen (2003) found that North American undergraduates reported that jealousy may be a sign of insecurity as well as a sign of love; equating jealousy with love can lead to the tacit acceptance of jealousy-related violence; jealousy-related violence might include emotional and sexual abuse of a wife by the husband. Violence in the context of a non-jealousy-related argument was judged negatively, whereas violence in the context of a jealousy-related argument resulted in the aggressing male being judged as more romantically loving his wife.

Individuals with high jealousy concerns are more likely to have less serotonin transporters (Marrazziti et al., 2003).

In general, individuals who perceive that their mate has left due to circumstances beyond anyone's control (e.g., accidental death) are less jealous compared to those who perceive their mate has left due to circumstances under his/her control (e.g., taking a job far away). A significantly higher level of jealousy was reported when it was perceived that the mate left the relationship for a rival, and this jealousy was raised to its highest level if the perception held that the rival was known (e.g., an acquaintance or friend); Marelich, 2002.

This corresponds with the findings of Bauerle et al. (2002) who proposed that jealousy is more likely when the cause is perceived as internal, controllable, and intentional.

Practical Application Exercise

The Add-On Skills
Responding to Meaning

SKILLS

Responding to Meaning

- Reflecting on Feeling and Reason
- Reflecting on Feeling and Meaning

Responding to Feeling

- Reflecting and Categorizing
- Determining Intensity
- Responding

Responding to Content

- Suspending Judgment
- Reflecting on Key Words/Phrases
- Paraphrsing Key Words/Phrases

SUBSKILLS

Sender	Receiver	Observers

Give the context.
 	
Provide several 30-second expressions.
 	
Provide feedback.
	Position
	Posture
	Observe
	Listen
	Pause and reflect
	(5WH)
	
	1. Respond: "You look _____."
	
	2. Respond to content: "What I hear you saying is _____."
	
	3. Respond to feeling: "You feel _____."
	
	4. Respond to feeling and meaning: "You feel _____ because _____."
		Observe the receiver's
		  Positioning
		  Posturing
		  Observing
		  Listening skills and
		    behaviors
		
		Write your own responses.
		
		Rate the receiver's responses.
		
		Provide feedback.

SENDERS: Do not provide expressions/statements that reveal personal content that might be embarrassing, intimate, or potentially harmful to yourself or others.

Asking Relevant Questions

The second responding skill is *asking questions*. You ask questions to get information so that you can manage or help. Crisp questions get answers without interrogating. Interrogation is often perceived as an interpersonal attack. People often put up a shield (get defensive) when they believe they are under attack. The components of this sub-skill are listed in Figure 13.

Figure 13. The Add-On Skills: Asking Relevant Questions

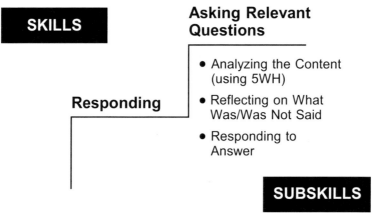

The Add-On Skills
Asking Relevant Questions

SKILLS

Asking Relevant Questions

Responding

- Analyzing the Content (using 5WH)
- Reflecting on What Was/Was Not Said
- Responding to Answer

SUBSKILLS

Getting good answers, even to crisp questions, takes skills. Your Basic Skills, as always, get you ready. Using your Add-On Skills helps you build the rapport you need to reduce any suspicion or resistance. You then select the most effective question to help fill your information gaps so that any action you take will be based on a more complete understanding. Questions asked in the context of caring and understanding should result in a higher probability of getting more reliable answers. Once you get a response (and the data you seek), you should respond to the person so that they know you heard them.

The Sub-Skills of Asking Questions

Analyzing the content/(5WH). The first component of asking questions is to *analyze the content* with the *5WH method*. Determining information and filling data gaps are imperative and selecting the appropriate 5WH can prove very useful in this effort.

Memorize the Who, What, When, Where, Why, and How System so that you can quickly analyze existing information. The more you use the 5WH, the more you will appreciate its usefulness. It is an invaluable skill for interpersonal management.

Reflecting on what was or was not said. The second component of asking questions is *reflecting on what was or was not said*. After the questions have been asked, reflect on the answer to see if you received the information your question sought. You frequently get a response after a question, but not the data you need to manage the situation. Practice reflecting so that you don't waste energy dealing with non-essential data. It is not implied that most people are trying to deceive you, but frequently they are interested in telling their version of an event and not providing the facts you need. Having a system will keep you on track. Using the responding sub-skills and components will allow you to ask the questions in a facilitative manner.

Responding to the answer. The third component of asking questions is *responding to the answer* (recycling). After you get an answer, you paraphrase the content (key words and phrases) back to the person who answered you to ensure you received what was sent. Again, this is "common sense" that many people don't have, and it can cause very serious problems. People give you answers and you fail to verbally confirm your understanding with them. You nod your head or grunt as an acknowledgment that you understood. The other person believes you understand them, and, of course, you know you did. But did you really? This is a major problem in communications of all sorts. Some say it is our self-concept that causes this reaction, but learning how to get the accurate information you need is vital.

Exercise 21: Reflection

After you read the situation below, reflect on the feeling and meaning, respond to the feeling and meaning using the sentence map, analyze what you saw and heard to determine what facts or details you need, ask an appropriate question, and reflect and paraphrase the answer.

> Your mate is sitting in a slumped posture in the den, head down, fingers cupped around the chin and mouth, staring vacantly at the floor. You make an innocuous inquiry and get the following response:
>
> "Oh it's nothing. It's just that I'm involved in a really big mess at the office. I really don't want to bother you with it. I just can't seem to figure out what to do."

Reflect on the Feeling and Meaning:

_____

_____

_____

Respond to the Feeling and Meaning:

(Person's name), you feel _____ because _____

_____

Reflect on the reply (5WH): What information do you have, and what information do you need?

_____

_____

_____

Ask an appropriate question (5WH):

_____

_____

_____

Reflect on the answer (recycle) and paraphrase:

_____

_____

_____

Practical Application Exercise

Your instructor will guide you through several role plays that will enhance your skills for asking relevant questions.

The Add-On Skills
Asking Relevant Questions

SKILLS

Asking Relevant Questions

Responding

- Analyzing the Content (using 5WH)
- Reflecting on What Was/Was Not Said
- Responding to Answer

- **To Content**
  - Suspending Judgment
  - Reflecting Key Words/ Phrases
  - Paraphrasing Key Words/Phrases

SUBSKILLS

- **To Feeling**
  - Reflecting and Categorizing
  - Determining Intensity
  - Responding

- **To Feeling and Meaning**
  - Reflecting on Feeling and Reason
  - Checking on Feeling and Meaning

Sender	Receiver	Observers

Make a 60-second statement regarding a life event that was significant to you.	Position
	Posture
	Observe
	Listen
	Pause and reflect (5WH)
		Observe the receiver's
		   Positioning
		   Posturing
		   Observing
		   Listening skills and
		      behaviors

Provide feedback.	Reflect on feeling and meaning. Respond to feeling and meaning: "You feel _____ because _____." Ask relevant questions: – Who – What – Where – Why – When – How Respond to answer: "You feel _____ because _____."	Write your own responses. Write your own questions. Rate the receiver's responses. Provide feedback.

SENDERS: Do not provide expressions/statements that reveal personal content that might be embarrassing, intimate, or potentially harmful to yourself or others.

Add-On Skill Set Summary

Now you are ready to tackle the main challenges of the management/supervision and interpersonal transactions that are inescapable in life—managing and interacting with difficult people. The goal is to "do for better, not for worse." "Better" means to be able to achieve your objectives with as little stress for you and the persons with whom you must and choose to interact. The Basic Skills and the Add-On Skill Sets are often useful communication management tools on their own merit. Many people perform better when they are treated with the "decency" that results from being managed or supervised with these skills. There are, however, a myriad of human transactions when more active involvement is the norm. In the next section of SoTelligence, you are shown how what you have learned applies to more active management and supervision.

The Add-On Skills
Communicating

Asking Relevant Questions

- Analyzing the Content (using 5WH)
- Reflecting on What Was/Was Not Said
- Responding to Answer

Responding

- **To Content**
  - Suspending Judgment
  - Reflecting Key Words/ Phrases
  - Paraphrasing Key Words/Phrases

- **To Feeling**
  - Reflecting and Categorizing
  - Determining Intensity
  - Responding

- **To Feeling and Meaning**
  - Reflecting on Feeling and Reason
  - Checking on Feeling and Meaning

Social Intelligence Skills

Module 5: The Application Skills Set

Managing Behavior

The challenges referred to in the summary of the Add-On Skill Set are the recurring, routine, or dominant situations associated with difficult people we must manage and interact with in our lives. Experience and research reveal that three skills are pertinent to managing situations with difficult people: handling requests, making requests, and reinforcing behaviors (Figure 14).

Figure 14. The Application Skills: Managing Behavior

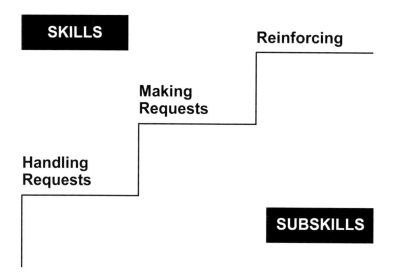

The Application Skills
Managing Behavior

SKILLS

Reinforcing

Making Requests

Handling Requests

SUBSKILLS

The first skill is handling the requests that are made of us. Most people are asked by others for significant amounts of information, direction, assistance, and permission on a regular basis. The skill of *handling requests* has been targeted to manage this theme.

The second skill is *making requests* of other people. We need assistance in receiving direction, information, and permission on a regular basis. In order to do that, we must make a request of someone.

The third skill that has been observed in transactions between persons is a reinforcing or rewarding behavior. It appears that each transaction between persons presents an opportunity for that experience to be pleasant (thus increasing the likelihood of a reoccurrence of the behavior) or unpleasant (thus diminishing the likelihood of occurrence). The skill to manage that theme is *reinforcing behavior.*

Handling Requests

Handling requests, the first skill of the Application Skills Set, involves listening to a request, then considering existing rules, human rights or ethics that may establish reasons for granting or denying the request. Care must be taken to be sure legitimate requests are granted and non-legitimate requests are denied. When this Application Skill is used with the Basic and Add-On Skill Sets, you will be managing and interacting with fairness and decency. Trust will be developed in those instances when requests are denied or delayed for further consideration. Persons may be disappointed at a request denial, but when interpersonal skill (decency) accompanies the response, neither party should experience significant stress from the event. See Figure 15.

Figure 15. The Application Skills: Handling Requests

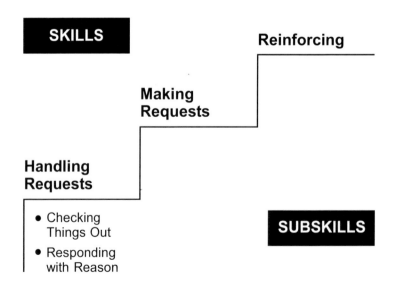

The Application Skills
Handling Requests

SKILLS

Reinforcing

Making
Requests

Handling
Requests

- Checking
  Things Out
- Responding
  with Reason

SUBSKILLS

Just as civil and criminal laws provide citizens freedom, so do fair rules and ethics add to the quality of our life. This includes our workplace and our homes. It has become obvious that rules work better when all affected have input into their development. Fair rules and observance of ethical standards are as critical to our business relationships. Earlier in SoTelligence, you listed the characteristics of a good manager and later the characteristics of a good communicator. These characteristics establish the age old ethic of informal rules that should always guide us in the absence of formal ones in our business transactions.

Examine one of the most important reasons for rules. Rules help de-personalize your actions. It's not you denying a request or granting a request. It's because a person is or is not entitled by rules or ethics that the request is granted or denied.

Exercise 22: Handling Requests

Think back to the last time one of your work-related requests was denied.

How did it make you feel?

_____

_____

_____

_____

_____

How did it affect your behavior or performance?

_____

_____

_____

_____

_____

The Sub-Skills of Handling Requests

Checking things out. The first sub-skill of handling requests is *checking things out*. Even if you ignore a request, an interpersonal consequence occurs and it's usually negative. When a request is made, use your Basic Skills and Add-On Skill Sets to "check things out." By listening carefully, asking specific questions (5WH), responding (paraphrasing) to the answers you receive (recycling), and knowing your rules and policies, you'll be able to handle requests skillfully.

Responding with reason. The second sub-skill of handling requests is *responding with reason*. Giving the reason eliminates the doubt that may occur about your fairness. Being fair communicates basic respect to others. Persons will be less likely to accuse you of partiality when you are open about your reasons for denying or granting a request. Giving reasons for your decisions reduces problems.

Three action choices are possible to a request. They are included with formats below:

"Yes, _____ because _____."

"No, _____ because _____."

Yes or no would be a result of policy or rules.

If you cannot respond by saying "Yes" or "No," you should respond by saying "I'm not sure." "I'm not sure" should be followed by the reason for the delay and the time you will be able to make the decision.

"I'm not sure _____ because _____."

Exercise 23: Handling a Request: Knowing the Rules

An employee makes the following request: "I know I have used up my personal leave time, but my wife's nephew has a layover here tomorrow, and I'd like the day off so I can go with her to the airport to pick him up and show him around town. How about it? You could knock off a day from next year's PTO allotment."

What things, if any, need to be checked out before this request is handled?

_____

_____

_____

_____

_____

_____

_____

How would you handle this request?

_____

_____

_____

_____

_____

_____

_____

What are the benefits/risks of granting this request?

_____

_____

_____

_____

_____

_____

Exercise 24: Handling a Request:
Responding with a Reason

List five "human rights" you believe people have.

1. _____

2. _____

3. _____

4. _____

5. _____

List three requests that might trouble you personally but you believe you would have to grant.

1. _____

2. _____

3. _____

After denying a request because it would have clearly been against the rules, the person denied becomes angry. What skill would first be most appropriate? Why?

_____

_____

_____

_____

After delaying a decision for a person, the person says, "So now it's the old run around. I guess you didn't think I would follow up on this, huh? Well you're not gonna play games with me!" What is your skilled response? Why?

_____

_____

_____

_____

_____

Practical Application Exercise

Your instructor will guide you through several role plays that will enhance your skills for handling requests.

The Application Skills
Handling Requests

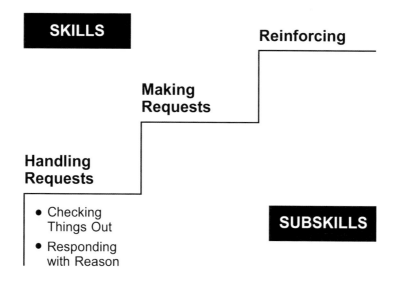

Sender	Receiver	Observers

Make a 30- to 60-second statement asking the receiver to do something for you.	Position
	Posture
	Observe
	Listen
	
	Handles request:
	
	— Responds to meaning: "You feel _____ because _____."
	
	— Asks relevant questions to help make decision (use 5WH format)
	
	— Responds to answer
	
	— Handles request:
	
	"Yes _____ because _____." OR
	
	"No _____ because _____." OR
	
	"Maybe _____ because _____ (and when you will give an answer)."
		Observe the receiver's:
		  Positioning
		  Posturing
		  Observing
		  Listening skills and
		    behaviors
		
		Write your own responses.
		
		Write your own questions.

SENDERS: Do not provide expressions/statements that reveal personal content that might be embarrassing, intimate, or potentially harmful to yourself or others.

                                           Social Intelligence Skills

Making Requests

Making requests is the second skill of the Application Skills Set. This is the skill that helps you get people to act, cooperate, and do things without intimidating them. The sub-skills for making a request are listed in Figure 16.

Figure 16. The Application Skills: Making Requests

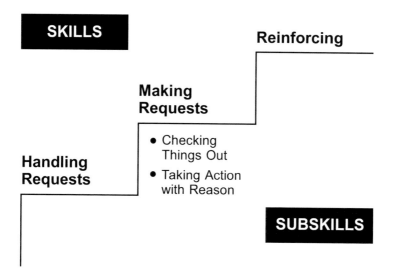

The Application Skills
Making Requests

SKILLS

Reinforcing

Making Requests

- Checking Things Out
- Taking Action with Reason

Handling Requests

SUBSKILLS

The Sub-Skills of Making Requests

Checking things out. The first sub-skill of making requests is *checking things out*. Use the Basic Skills and Add-On Skill sets when making requests just as you would for handling requests. To prepare yourself, review the possible questions that may arise, any feelings that you might encounter, and any resistance you might experience. Having memorized the 5WH will allow you to employ the system and, by putting yourself in the other person's place, you can anticipate much of what might happen. If you have a good relationship with the person involved, all of this may sound far too complex, so simply make your request with decency and respect.

Taking action with a reason. The second sub-skill of making requests is *taking action with a reason*. How a request is made is often as important as the request itself. Taking action includes being specific:

What do you want? (quantity)
When do you want it? (time) and
Why do you want it? (be specific)

If anything goes amiss, you have your Basic Skills and Add-On Skill sets to bail you out.

Respectful formats are useful in making requests.

"Would you please_____?"

"Please_____?"

"I would appreciate it if_____?"

These formats generally get the best results. This is how most of us would like to be asked to do something, respectfully and with specificity. If you set the standard of decency in making requests by modeling, it's very difficult to ignore, just as it is when people are indecent when making requests. If you are, however, in a situation where responsibility is being ignored or danger may result if behavior is not changed or instructions are not followed, you may have to use stronger formats and outline consequences; "Leave this area at once!" "Leave this area at once or I will call security!" As you check things out (size up a situation) you may determine that strong action is necessary.

> If you set the standard of decency in making requests by modeling, it's very difficult to ignore, just as it is when people are indecent when making requests of you.

Be concrete and behavioral.

MILD
"Would you mind (request) because (reason)."

MODERATE
"I want you to (request) because (reason)."

STRONG
"I want you to (request) because (reason), and if you do not (request), I will (consequence)."

Exercise 25: Taking Action

You have a business deadline to meet and something unforeseen has happened that is going to make meeting it close. The only employee around is someone you really don't know well, but you need some help. Formulate a request of this person to get some assistance.

_____

_____

_____

_____

You need to ask your secretary for information to complete a report that you will present during a staff conference tomorrow morning. You cannot otherwise obtain the information. Formulate a request to get the assistance you need.

_____

_____

_____

_____

Practical Application Exercise

Your instructor will guide you through several role plays that will enhance your skills for making requests.

The Application Skills
Making Requests

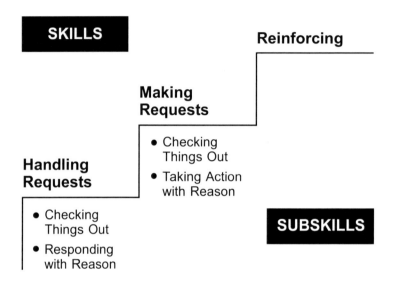

SKILLS

Reinforcing

Making Requests

- Checking Things Out
- Taking Action with Reason

Handling Requests

- Checking Things Out
- Responding with Reason

SUBSKILLS

Sender	Receiver	Observers
Give the context. Role play inappropriate behavior. Provide feedback.	Position Posture Observe Listen Check things out Respond to feeling and meaning Make a request Use all skills as necessary	Observe the receiver's: Positioning Posturing Observing Listening skills and behaviors Write your own responses Write your own questions Write your own request Rate the receiver's action(s) and reason(s) Provide feedback

SENDERS: Do not provide expressions/statements that reveal personal content that might be embarrassing, intimate, or potentially harmful to yourself or others.

Reinforcing

Reinforcing behavior, the third and final skill of the Application Skills Set, is the skill of administering rewards to increase or maintain desired behaviors and establishing consequences to reduce or eliminate undesirable behaviors. The administration of consequences is often referred to as punishment. Reinforcement and punishment may be verbal or nonverbal, and each can be administered in a positive or negative way.

Figure 17. The Application Skills: Reinforcing

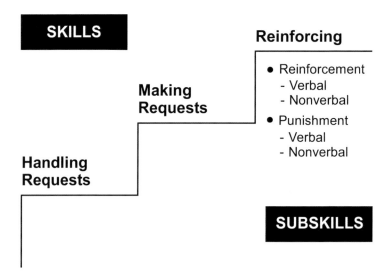

One of the most accepted explanations of why humans behave as they do is tied to reinforcement theories. We tend to become habituated (repeated behavior) because of tension reduction (pleasure) following certain actions. There are several theories of behavior and some are quite complicated. The reinforcement theory is, however, generally accepted as the model for how humans learn. The theory will be simplified here for use in a management and communication context.

As with all of the skills in this manual, you must be sensitive to the culture and social group you are working within so as *not* to offend or embarrass anyone.

The Sub-Skills of Reinforcing

Reinforcement. As was mentioned earlier, reinforcement is intended to increase or maintain desired behaviors. Social reward appears to be the most powerful in shaping human behavior, and they are readily available. Reinforcement may be done verbally or nonverbally. In effective management, the goal is to either observe people very closely so that your positive rewards can be administered for the desired behavior or arrange the circumstances that encourage the behavior you're after so that it can be rewarded in a timely manner.

Verbal reinforcement. There are several ways we can verbally reinforce desired behaviors. Saying thank you when your roommate cleans the kitchen or rewarding a child with "Great job" when they've cleaned a room without being told are examples of verbal reinforcement. Of course, these are examples of polite and positive interactions. Sometimes people say something with the intention of increasing or maintaining a desired behavior, but they do so in a negative way. Consider the case where an employee completes a rigorous and complicated report on time and proudly hands it to the boss only to hear, "Thanks for doing your job." These attempts at reinforcing often have the opposite effect.

Nonverbal reinforcement. Nonverbal reinforcement involves the use of gestures to maintain or increase a desired behavior. A smile, a pat on the back, a hug, and a wink are all positive gestures. Here, again, some people attempt to reinforce by doing negative gestures. Imagine you are an employee turning in a required report, and when you hand it to your supervisor, the supervisor literally snatches the report out of your hand, places it on a pile without looking at it, and never makes eye contact with you. The intent may be to impress on you what a busy person he/she is, but most people will walk away from that interaction with a negative feeling toward the boss.

Here are some examples of reinforcement:

Example #1: Verbal Reinforcer:

You make a special request of a colleague (or employee) to come in to work early because you need his/her help in getting a project completed by the deadline. You say,

> "I really appreciate you coming to work a little early today to help me meet this deadline. I could not have done it without your help."

Example #2: Nonverbal Reinforcer:

> You come home from grocery shopping to find your significant other making dinner.
>
> > Give your partner a hug and a kiss on the cheek.

Punishment. The second sub-skill of reinforcing behavior is punishment, sometimes referred to as *giving negative reinforcement*. Punishment, or negative reinforcement, refers to those actions or words that are intended to reduce or eliminate another person's undesirable behavior. Punishment works, although not as powerfully as positive reinforcement. In this context, "works" means that these strategies are effective in getting persons to behave more responsibly (according to the rules or standards). Negative reinforcers followed by positive reinforcers seem to be vey effective. For example, a parent tells his/her child, "TV time is over, it's study time now." After the child turns the TV off and begins to study, the parent says, "Thanks for doing that so promptly without any complaints." This "compound interaction" is much more effective than just directing the child to turn off the television and do his/her homework.

In general, punishment (i.e., negative reinforcement) means removing privileges, restricting normal freedoms, and withholding rewards in response to inappropriate behavior. There are two ways to deliver the reinforcers, verbally and nonverbally.

Verbal punishment. Verbally, you choose words and expressions that are positive or negative and link them to the behaviors that you wish others to use or discontinue. Words and phrases like, "Stop that!" or "Knock it off!" as well as insults or hurtful statements are all examples of verbal punishers.

Nonverbal punishment. Nonverbal expressions of reinforcement may be even more important than verbal. Research contends that a very large number of the important messages we send and receive are non-verbal. Cues like expressions (e.g., a glaring and angry expression), gestures (e.g., thumbs down), posture (e.g., weight positioned on the back foot and arms crossed), and distance (e.g., standing further away than 8 feet) are examples. Our words may signify approval when our body language does not. The message is, at best, confusing.

What's good about punishment? It's effective if delivered in the right dose *immediately following* the undesired behavior. It's usually fast. It may have beneficial side effects.

What are the problems with punishment? Acute traumas do not twist or warp personalities in the same way as chronic punishment (and the attempt to reinforce with negative feedback). Logical painful consequences from undesired behaviors are *sometimes* better teachers than our attempts to scare, intervene, or otherwise dissuade. Here are some of the well-known and well-documented problems with punishment:

- Escape–the ultimate response can be suicide.

- Aggression–the person may become aggressive and look for alternative ways to perform the undesired behavior.

- Apathy–the person may develop a "defeated" attitude that can generalize quickly to other behaviors.

- Abuse–punishment can easily turn into abuse.

- Modeling–the person may imitate the punisher and "pass it on."

- Ethics–there are many debates regarding the ethics of punishment.

- Chronic punishment (and the attempt to reinforce with negative feedback) may result in low self-esteem as well as the avoidance of punishment at any cost.

Exercise 26: Reinforcement and Punishment

Answer the following items as they would apply to the context of the *workplace* and *home*.

List three verbal reinforcers you can use in the *workplace*.

1. _____

2. _____

3. _____

List three nonverbal reinforcers you can use in the *workplace*.

1. _____

2. _____

3. _____

List three verbal punishers you can use in the **workplace**.

1. _____
2. _____
3. _____

List three nonverbal punishers you can use in the **workplace**.

1. _____
2. _____
3. _____

List three verbal reinforcers you can use in the **home**.

1. _____
2. _____
3. _____

List three nonverbal reinforcers you can use in the **home**.

1. _____
2. _____
3. _____

List three verbal punishers you can use in the **home**.

1. _____
2. _____
3. _____

List three nonverbal punishers you can use in the **home**.

1. _____
2. _____
3. _____

Practical Application Exercise

Your instructor will guide you through several role plays that will enhance your reinforcing skills.

The Application Skills
Reinforcing

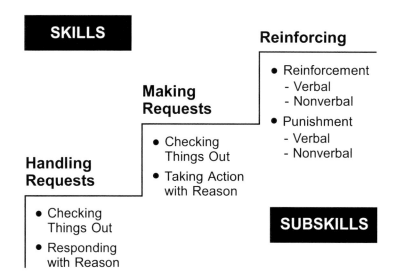

Sender	Receiver	Observers
Give the context. Role play an incident that clearly needs reinforcement. Provide feedback.	Position Posture Observe Listen Check things out. Respond to feeling and meaning. Ask questions if needed. Reinforce verbally or nonverbally. Make a request. Uses all skills as necessary.	Observe the receiver's Positioning Posturing Observing Listening skills and behaviors Write your own reinforcement. Rate the receiver's reinforcement. Provide feedback.

SENDERS: Do not provide expressions/statements that reveal personal content that might be embarrassing, intimate, or potentially harmful to yourself or others.

Application Skills Set Summary

The focus of this training is to share with you the interpersonal skills that will assist you in the management and supervision of those with whom you interact, whether in your work with employees and your supervisors or in personal transactions such as with family and acquaintances. The skills are generic. You provide the context with how you live your life. If you wish to reduce your stress and take more control of your life so it is better and not worse, apply these skills because they are life skills. The more you practice these skills, the more you will like about yourself and grow in both your professional and personal development.

The Application Skills
Managing Behavior

SKILLS

Reinforcing

- Reinforcement
  - Verbal
  - Nonverbal
- Punishment
  - Verbal
  - Nonverbal

Making Requests

- Checking Things Out
- Taking Action with Reason

Handling Requests

- Checking Things Out
- Responding with Reason

SUBSKILLS

Module 6: Skills Activity

Skills Activity

Let's begin your practical application of the Basic, Add-On, and Application Skills sets. Your instructor will present you with a role-play scenario in which an employee requires counseling for a work-related problem. But first let's review each skill set and their sub-skills and components.

The Basic Skills
Sizing Up the Situation

Listening
- Suspending Judgment
- Identifying Key Words/Phrases
- Identifying Intensity
- Determining Mood

SKILLS

Observing
- Looking Carefully
- Making Inferences
- Typical vs. Atypical
- Stress vs. No Stress

Posturing
- Erect Posture
- Forward Lean
- Eliminating Distracting Behaviors

Positioning
- Distancing
- Facing Squarely
- Looking Directly

SUBSKILLS

Arranging
- Eliminating Distractions
- Adding Attractors

The Add-On Skills
Communicating

Asking Relevant Questions

- Analyzing the Content (using 5WH)
- Reflecting on What Was/Was Not Said
- Responding to Answer

Responding

- **To Content**
  - Suspending Judgment
  - Reflecting Key Words/ Phrases
  - Paraphrasing Key Words/Phrases

- **To Feeling**
  - Reflecting and Categorizing
  - Determining Intensity
  - Responding

- **To Feeling and Meaning**
  - Reflecting on Feeling and Reason
  - Checking on Feeling and Meaning

Social Intelligence Skills

The Application Skills
Managing Behavior

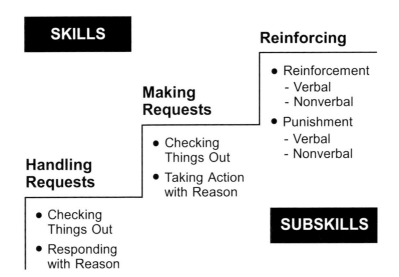

Using all of the components of the scenario, address each of the following skills and sub-skills. As you go through the exercise, note how each skill is important to the interaction.

The Basic Skills: Sizing Up the Situation

Arranging

Eliminating distractions: _____

_____

Adding attractions: _____

_____

Positioning

Distancing: _____

_____

Facing squarely: _____

_____

Looking directly: _____

_____

Posturing

Sitting/standing erect: _____

_____

Leaning slightly forward: _____

_____

Eliminating distracting behaviors: _____

_____

Observing

Looking carefully: _____

_____

Making inferences: _____

_____

Deciding typical or atypical: _____

_____

Deciding stress or no stress: _____

_____

Listening

Suspending judgment: _____

_____

Identifying key words/phrases: _____

_____

Identifying intensity of expression: _____

_____

Determining mood: _____

_____

The Add-On Skills: Communicating

Responding to Content

Suspending judgment: _____

_____

Reflecting on key words and phrases: _____

_____

Paraphrasing key words and phrases: _____

_____

Responding to Feeling

Reflecting and categorizing: _____

_____

Determining intensity: _____

_____

Responding: _____

_____

Responding to Feeling and Meaning

Reflecting on feeling and reason: _____

_____

Reflecting on and meaning: _____

_____

Asking Relevant Questions

Analyzing content: _____

_____

Choosing 5WH: _____

_____

Reflecting on what was or was not said: _____

_____

Responding to the answer: _____

_____

The Application Skills: Managing Behavior

Handling Requests

Checking things out: _____

_____

Responding with a reason: _____

_____

Making Requests

Checking things out: _____

_____

Taking action with a reason: _____

_____

Reinforcing

Verbal reinforcement: _____

_____

Nonverbal reinforcement: _____

_____

Verbal punishment: _____

_____

Nonverbal punishment: _____

_____

Appendix:
Exercises and Answer Sheets

This section contains answer sheets and activities that may be introduced and explained during classroom training.

Intellectual Skills: IQ Test
Answer Sheet

I. Verbal (English)

1. (ORE)	(ONE)	(ATE)	(INK)
2. (ROW)	(BAR)	(TAR)	(MOW)
3. (SLIP)	(SLAP)	(SLAM)	(SLEW)
4. (REP/RIP)	(OWN/ONE)	(ALL/ALE)	(OWL/ILL)

II. Quantification (Mathematics)

5. 28	33	16	19
6. 4	6	8	10
7. 160	45	25	100
8. 25	30	35	40

III. Spatial Visual

9. (1)	(2)	(3)	(4)	(5)	(6)
10. (1)	(2)	(3)	(4)	(5)	(6)
11. (1)	(2)	(3)	(4)	(5)	(6)
12. (1)	(2)	(3)	(4)	(5)	(6)

Scoring for Intellectual Skills Exercise:

One correct answer	90 - 100
Two correct answers	101 - 109
Three correct answers	110 - 119
Four correct answers	120 - 129
Five correct answers	130 - 135
Six correct answers	136 - 140
Seven correct answers	141 - 145
Eight correct answers	146 - 150
Nine correct answers	151 - 155
Ten correct answers	156 - 160

Do not read too much into these results! You would need to take an actual IQ test with several questions to determine your true IQ.

Intellectual Skills: SAT Questions
Verbal and Comprehension

1. A story's meaning is often obvious—that is, stated directly but sometimes it is often _____.

    a) simple   b) climatic   c) implied   d) altruistic

2. San Francisco is a cosmopolitan city, and having several newspapers in many languages reflects its _____ population.

    a) homogenous   b) heterogeneous   c) insular   d) literal

3. Even after devouring their picnic lunch, the children were still _____ and begging for more.

    a) gladden   b) embellished   c) gully   d) covetous

4. The scientists who breed nearly extinct bird species refer to their outdoor enclosures that house the birds as _____.

    a) arboretums   b) depots   c) aviaries   d) nests

5. Which one of the following does not belong with the others?

    a) candle   b) lamp   c) sun   d) lighter

6. The United States congress has the power to _____ an elected official charged with a major crime.

    a) convict   b) exonerate   c) veto   d) impeach

7. Celebrities often see themselves as _____ figures to whom ordinary moral _____ do not necessarily apply.

    a) redundant...rules   b) pedagogical...enticements
    c) gifted...benefits   d) privileged...constraints

8. Government officials charged that a food producer had engaged in _____ practices by misleading consumers on the nutritional quality of their product.

    a) inordinate   b) illegitimate   c) deceptive   d) exacting

(continued)

Intellectual Skills: SAT Questions
Verbal and Comprehension (concluded)

9. When a person continues to suppress their impulse to complain whether vexation is _____ or grave they will appear to be Automatons, _____ of emotion.

   a) severe; benefit
   c) trivial; devoid of

   b) deserving; incapable of
   d) frivolous; consumed by

10. The consequences of the conspirators' _____ caused severe punishment for all other alleged conspirators.

   a) machinations   b) rumination   c) consultation   d) forebodings

Intellectual Skills: SAT Questions
Mathematics

1. Which one of the following does not belong?

   a) 3/9　　　　　b) 4/8　　　　　c) 2/4　　　　　d) 2/7

2. How much is 10 x 10 x 0?

   a) 30　　　　　b) 1,000　　　　　c) 0　　　　　d) 10,000

3. Which one of the following comes next at the end of this row of letters: XOOXXOOOXXXOOOO?

   a) XXOOOOO　　b) XXXX0000　　c) XXOOO　　d) XXXX00000

4. How much is double one-half times three quarters?

   a) 2¾　　　　　b) ¾　　　　　c) 1¾　　　　　d) 2

5. There are 10 boxes of donuts on a shelf and each box contains the same number of donuts. If 3 of the boxes contain a total of 36 donuts, how many donuts are there in the other 7 boxes?

   a) 70　　　　　b) 84　　　　　c) 104　　　　　d) 124

6. In the number 0.487, which of the following does the number 7 represent?

   a) 7 x 1/10　　b) 7 x 1/100　　c) 7 x 1/1000　　d) 7 x 1/10,000

7. Which number would follow in the pattern 6, 9, 15, 24:

   a) 49　　　　　b) 30　　　　　c) 21　　　　　d) 36

8. Which of the following fractions is least?

   a) 11/12　　　　b) 3/8　　　　c) 8/9　　　　d) 5/9

9. Which of the following sales commission is greatest?

   a) 1% of $1,000　　b) 10% of $200　　c) 15% of $100　　d) 25% of $40

10. If Q/5 = F, then Q/10 = _____

    a) 10F　　　　b) 2F　　　　c) F/2　　　　d) F/10

Tuff Jobs

	1 YOUR Ranking	2 TEAM Ranking	3 OSHA Ranking	4 Diff. bet. 1 & 3	5 Diff. bet. 2 & 3
Agriculture worker					
Police officer					
Deep sea diver					
Construction worker					
Rancher					
Welder					
Chemical worker					
Miner					
Trawler worker					
Firefighter					
TOTAL SCORES					
				YOUR Score	TEAM Score

1 = Toughest in terms of physical injury
10 = Least tough in terms of physical injury

SCORING for Columns 4 or 5: Take the TOTAL SCORE for that column, multiply it by 2; subtract that answer from 100. This is your percentage of agreement.

Source: OSHA

Visual Recollection Exercise 1

Purpose: To understand how accurately you visually recall the common-place world.

Directions: This is a timed test (6 minutes). Please place your answer to the left of the number; you are encouraged to guess.

bottom   1. On a standard traffic light, is the green on the top or bottom?

right   2. In which hand is the Statue of Liberty's torch?

clock   3. Does a merry-go-round turn counterclockwise or clockwise?

_0 & ✳ (1)_   4. What two digits on a telephone are not accompanied by letters?

left   5. When you walk, does your right arm swing with your right leg or your left leg?

_20_   6. How many matches are in a standard pack?

red   7. On the American flag, is the uppermost stripe red or white?

_86.6_   8. What is the lowest number on an FM radio dial?

_____ 9. On the back of a dollar bill, what is in the center?

Clockwise   10. Which direction do the blades on a fan rotate for cooling?

_____ 11. Whose face is on a dime?

_8_   12. How many sides does a stop sign have?

left   13. Do books have their even-numbered pages on the left or right?

_6_   14. How many lug nuts are on a standard American car wheel?

_7_   15. How many sides are there on a standard pencil?

(continued)

Visual Recollection Exercise 1 (concluded)

_8_ 16. How many hot dog buns are in a standard package?

left 17. On which side of a standard Venetian blind is the cord (or wand) that adjusts the opening between the slats?

_4 (3)_ 18. How many curves are there in a standard paper clip?

joker 19. On which playing card is the card maker's trademark?

_Y_ 20. On a standard computer keyboard, over which number is the # symbol?

Observation Skills Exercise 1

T (F) 1. The clock shows the time to be 1:15.

T (F) 2. Five people are wearing hats.

(T) F 3. There is a baby.

T (F) 4. There are five women.

(T) F 5. One of the men standing has one hand in his pocket.

T (F) 6. Someone is wearing glasses.

T (F) 7. There are 11 people present.

T (F) 8. The woman holding the baby is wearing a hat.

(T) F 9. Someone is holding a newspaper.

(T) F 10. One man has a mustache.

Observation Skills Exercise 2

(T)   F   1. The man wearing a yellow shirt has his hands in his pocket.

T   (F)   2. There are two small children sitting in the front row.

T   (F)   3. A blue and yellow gazebo stands in the background.

(T)   F   F   4. The crowd is cheering.

(T)   F   5. There is a man standing with his arms crossed.

T   (F)   6. One chair in the front row is empty.

(T)   F   7. There is a woman wearing a sweatshirt and blue jeans holding a jacket.

(T)   F   8. A man has his arm raised above his head.

(T)   F   9. There is a young girl with her eyes closed.

T   (F)   10. A child is crying.

(T)   F   11. There is a woman wearing a pink shift.

T   (F)   12. A man is using a video camera.

(T)   F   13. Someone is eating or drinking.

T   (F)   14. A woman in the front row has her legs crossed.

(T)   F   15. The crowd is near a wooded area.

(T)   F   16. A woman on the second row is crouching.

(T)   F   17. People are sitting on metal folding chairs.

T   (F)   18. A man and woman are arguing.

T   (F)   19. The weather is cold.

(T)   F   20. All the men sitting on chairs are wearing glasses.

Comprehension Test 1

1. Each country has its own "Independence Day"; do you have a 4th of July in England? *Yes*

2. How many birthdays does the average man have? *one*

3. Can a man living in Winston-Salem, NC, be buried west of the Mississippi? *no*

4. If you only had one match and entered a room in which there was a kerosene lamp, an oil heater, and a wood burning stove, which would you light first? *lamp (the match)*

5. Some months have 30 days, some have 31. How many have 28? *one* *All*

6. If a doctor gave you three pills and told you to take one every half hour, how long would the pills last? *1 hour* *1 ½ hours*

7. A house is built so that each side has a southern exposure. If a bear were to wander by the house, mostly likely, what color would the bear be? *black (white)*

8. I have in my hand two U.S. coins that total 55 cents in value. One is not a nickel. What are the two coins? *1 nickel ¢ ½ dollar*

9. A farmer has 17 sheep. All but 9 died. How many does he have left? *9*

10. Two men play chess. They played five games and each man won the same number of games. There were no ties. How can this be? *played other people*

11. Take two apples from three apples and what do you get? *2 apples* *1 apple*

12. Divide 30 by ½ and add 10. What's the answer? *(70)* *25*

13. If your room were pitch dark and you needed a matching pair of socks, how many socks would you need to take out of the bureau drawer if there are 26 white and 25 blue? *3*

Comprehension Test 1 (concluded)

14. If it takes 10 men 10 days to dig a hole, how long will it take five men to dig half a hole? *(no ½ hole)*

15. How many animals did Moses take on the Ark? *(Noah did)*

16. A doctor refuses to operate on a patient who has been injured in an auto accident in which the patient's father was killed. The doctor refuses to operate because the patient is the doctor's son. How can this be? *(it's his mom)*

17. There are 12 one-cent stamps in a dozen, but how many two-cent stamps are there in a dozen? *(12)*

18. What four words appear on every denomination of U.S. coin and currency? *(In God we Trust)* *United States of America*

19. Which is correct: 7 and 8 are 13 or 7 and 8 is 13? *(it's 15)*

20. If 3 cats kill 3 rats in 3 minutes, how long will it take for 100 cats to kill 100 rats? *(3 min)*

Listening Skills Exercise
"Dinner at 5"

All Questionable

Read the following statements and rate each statement as:

      T = True
      F = False
      Q = Questionable (You don't have enough information to
            determine if it's definitely True or False.)

1. A man bought a lobster.   T   F   **(Q)**

2. A young woman ate dinner with a man.   T   **(F)**   Q

3. The couple ate dinner at 5 o'clock.   T   F   **(Q)**

4. The man was a biker.   **(T)**   F   Q

5. The man has a beard.   T   **(F)**   Q

6. The woman was young.   T   F   **(Q)**

7. The man stole the woman's necklace.   **(T)**   F   Q

8. The woman and man were yelling at each other.   T   F   **(Q)**

9. The necklace broke when it was pulled from the   T   F   **(Q)**
     woman's neck.

10. The woman chased the man from the bar.   T   **(F)**   Q

Listening Skills Exercise
"The Witness Statement"

Read the witness's statement:

"I saw this businessman turn off the lights in the store when a man appeared and demanded money. The owner opened a cash register. The contents of the cash register were scooped up, and the man sped away. I notified a member of the police force promptly."

Answer the following:

    T = True
    F = False
    Q = Questionable (You don't have enough information to determine if it's definitely True or False.)

1. A man appeared after the owner had turned off his store lights.　　　　　T　F　**Q**

2. The robber was a man.　　　　　T　F　**Q**

3. The man did not demand money.　　　　　T　F　**Q**

4. The man who opened the cash register was the the owner.　　　　　T　F　**Q**

5. The store owner scooped up the contents of the cash register and ran away.　　　　　T　F　Q

6. Someone opened a cash register.　　　　　**T**　F　Q

7. After the man who demanded the money scooped up the contents of the cash register, he ran away.　　　　　T　F　**Q**

8. While the cash register contained money, the story does not say how much.　　　　　T　F　**Q**

9. The contents of the cash register were taken out of the cash register.　　　　　**T**　F　Q

10. The police department was contacted right away.　　　　　T　F　**Q**

11. The person who demanded money was a man.　　　　　**T**　F　Q

12. The owner of the store was a man.　　　　　T　F　**Q**

How Many Squares Do You See?

Verbal Intelligence Index

Rate each of the verbal statements given to each of the following possible scenarios by placing a checkmark (✓) in the appropriate box. Use the following five-point rating scale:

$$5 = \text{Very Effective}$$
$$4 = \text{Effective}$$
$$3 = \text{Neutral}$$
$$2 = \text{Fair}$$
$$1 = \text{Poor}$$

You may give the same rating to several options.

Assessing Your Verbal Intelligence

Business Scenario #1

You are a manager of a large group. Your foreman is very competent and has been with the company for many years. You are forced to discipline him for a minor transgression. In the midst of the discussion he says, "I think I've had about all of this company I can stand. Maybe it's time for me to just move on down the road."

5 = Very Effective
4 = Effective
3 = Neutral
2 = Fair
1 = Poor

	5	4	3	2	1	Expert	Differ.
We all have to do what we have to do.	☐	☐	☐	☑	☐	1	1
That's fine with me.	☐	☐	☐	☐	☑	1	0
You are obviously too upset to talk right now.	☐	☑	☐	☐	☐	3	1
You need to get in touch with reality.	☐	☐	☐	☐	☑	1	0
Why don't we both calm down and talk later.	☐	☑	☐	☐	☐	4	0
I don't think it's worth ending our relationship. Let's work on it.	☐	☑	☐	☐	☐	5	1
SCORE							3

Take your total "difference" points, multiply them by 4, and subtract this result from 100. This is your percentage.

$$\begin{array}{r} 3 \\ \times 4 \\ \hline 12 \end{array} \qquad \begin{array}{r} 100 \\ -12 \\ \hline 88 \end{array}$$

Business Scenario #2

You are an employee who arrived to work 20 minutes late. You did not call in because you got caught in traffic and your cell phone had lost its charge. Your supervisor approaches you as you enter your place of work and says, "If you're going to be late, at least call. That's company policy."

5 = Very Effective
4 = Effective
3 = Neutral
2 = Fair
1 = Poor

	5	4	3	2	1	Expert	Differ.
Sorry, it won't happen again.	☐	☐	☐	☑	☐	4	2
Will you lighten up?	☐	☐	☐	☐	☑	1	0
I was stuck in traffic.	☐	☐	☐	☑	☐	3	1
I know you are concerned, but traffic was bad.	☐	☐	☑	☐	☐	5	2
I couldn't help it.	☐	☐	☐	☐	☑	2	1
I hear you.	☐	☐	☐	☐	☑	1	0
SCORE							6

x4

Take your total "difference" points, multiply them by 4, and subtract this result from 100. This is your percentage.

Assessing Your Verbal Intelligence

Personal Relationship Scenario #1

Your spouse says to you as you're leaving the house, "I really care about you. I hope you're feeling the same about me."

5 = Very Effective
4 = Effective
3 = Neutral
2 = Fair
1 = Poor

	5	4	3	2	1	Expert	Differ.
That's good. Thanks!	☐	☐	☐	☐	☑	1	0
I really care about you.	☐	☑	☐	☐	☐	5	1
It's nice to hear you feel that way.	☐	☐	☐	☑	☐	3	1
Look, that's great. I'll see you tonight.	☐	☐	☐	☐	☑	1	0
We'll talk about it when I get home.	☐	☐	☐	☐	☑	1	0
The feeling is mutual. See you later.	☐	☐	☑	☐	☐	3	0
SCORE							92

Take your total "difference" points, multiply them by 4, and subtract this result from 100. This is your percentage.

Personal Relationship Scenario #2

Your spouse says to you, "I wish we could spend a little more time together. I know we haven't been getting along like we should, but a lot of it is your fault."

You would immediately say...

5 = Very Effective
4 = Effective
3 = Neutral
2 = Fair
1 = Poor

	5	4	3	2	1	Expert	Differ.
Wait a minute! I think you have a lot to do with it.	☐	☐	☐	☐	☑	1	0
I'm sorry, but I don't agree.	☑	☐	☐	☐	☐	3	2
I appreciate you want to be with me more. How do you think we can fix it?	☑	☐	☐	☐	☐	5	0
I feel the same way sometimes.	☐	☐	☐	☑	☐	3	1
When you're ready to accept your part of the blame, I'll be glad to spend more time with you.	☐	☐	☐	☐	☑	1	0
What am I doing wrong?	☐	☐	☐	☑	☐	4	2
SCORE							5

Take your total "difference" points, multiply them by 4, and subtract this result from 100. This is your percentage.

Emotional Wisdom
(*Intra*personal)

Use the following scale to answer these questions:

5 = Strongly Agree
4 = Agree
3 = Neutral
2 = Disagree
1 = Strongly Disagree

_____ 1. I can name my feelings.

_____ 2. I've learned a lot about myself by listening to my feelings.

_____ 3. I am aware of my feelings most of the time.

_____ 4. I can tell when I am getting upset.

_____ 5. When I am sad, I know the reason(s) why.

_____ 6. I tend to judge myself by how I think others see me.

_____ 7. I enjoy my emotional life.

_____ 8. People who show a lot of strong emotion scare me.

_____ 9. I often wish I were someone else.

_____ 10. I pay attention to my physical state to understand my feelings.

_____ 11. I accept my feelings as my own.

_____ 12. I avoid situations that make me feel uncomfortable.

_____ 13. I avoid people who make me anxious.

_____ 14. I feel hurt when I've been criticized unjustly.

_____ 15. When I've made a mistake that other people notice, I don't feel embarrassed.

_____ **TOTAL YOUR SCORE**

Scoring:

65 – 75	Excellent
55 – 64	Good
45 – 54	Average
44 or less	Needs Improvement

Emotional Wisdom
(*Inter*personal)

Use the following scale to answer these questions:

5 = Strongly Agree
4 = Agree
3 = Neutral
2 = Disagree
1 = Strongly Disagree

_____ 1. In interacting with others, I can sense how they are feeling.

_____ 2. I can recognize emotions in others by watching their eyes.

_____ 3. I find it difficult to talk to people who do not share my views.

_____ 4. I focus on people's positive qualities.

_____ 5. I rarely have the urge to tell someone off.

_____ 6. I think about how others might feel before I give my opinion.

_____ 7. No matter with whom I am speaking, I am always a good listener.

_____ 8. I can sense the mood of a group when I walk into a room.

_____ 9. I can get new people I meet to talk about themselves.

_____ 10. I am good at "reading between the lines" when someone is talking.

_____ 11. I can usually tell how others feel about me.

_____ 12. I can sense someone's feelings even if they are unspoken.

_____ 13. I change my emotional expression depending on the person I am with.

_____ 14. I can tell when someone close to me is upset.

_____ 15. I feel bad when people are angry at me.

_____ **TOTAL YOUR SCORE**

Scoring:

65 – 75	Excellent
55 – 64	Good
45 – 54	Average
44 or less	Needs Improvement

Faces

1.
   a. anxious
   b. puzzled
   c. hurt
   d. aggravated

2.
   a. annoyed
   b. bold
   c. perturbed
   d. relieved

3.
   a. stuck
   b. hopeless
   c. crushed
   d. disappointed

4.
   a. impatient
   b. down
   c. bitter
   d. cross

5.
   a. grieved
   b. mad
   c. crushed
   d. bewildered

6.
   a. able
   b. powerful
   c. turned-on
   d. good

7.
   a. irritated
   b. outraged
   c. frightened
   d. empowered

8.
   a. content
   b. sorry
   c. annoyed
   d. exhausted

9.
   a. perplexed
   b. powerful
   c. fearless
   d. pleased

10.
    a. nervous
    b. spent
    c. poised
    d. satisfied

11.
    a. exhausted
    b. adequate
    c. relaxed
    d. aggressive

12.
    a. worried
    b. powerless
    c. inadequate
    d. jumpy

13.
    a. pleased
    b. powerful
    c. surprised
    d. dazed

14.
    a. unsure
    b. uncertain
    c. ready
    d. uptight

15.
    a. uneasy
    b. joyful
    c. forceful
    d. potent

16.
    a. shaken
    b. doubtful
    c. impatient
    d. powerless

Faces (concluded)

17.
    a. disoriented
    b. hesitant
    c. hurt
    d. alone

22.
    a. incensed
    b. determined
    c. defensive
    d. blue

18.
    a. steady
    b. cautious
    c. furious
    d. content

23.
    a. hopeful
    b. joyful
    c. bewildered
    d. surprised

19.
    a. insecure
    b. dismayed
    c. puzzled
    d. aggravated

24.
    a. impatient
    b. pulled
    c. confused
    d. hurting

20.
    a. heartsick
    b. vigorous
    c. frightened
    d. worried

25.
    a. confused
    b. angry
    c. scared
    d. disgusted

21.
    a. scared
    b. doubtful
    c. uneasy
    d. outraged

Feeling Word Matrix

Category	High Intensity	Moderate Intensity	Low Intensity
Happy	excited thrilled ecstatic elated	cheerful optimistic upbeat delighted	pleased glad satisfied fine
Sad	hopeless crushed miserable devastated	dejected dismayed hurt forlorn	down blue low somber
Scared	panicked petrified fearful terrified	worried anxious shaky tense	startled hesitant uneasy edgy
Angry	outraged furious hostile hateful	aggravated irritated mad offended	perturbed annoyed hassled bothered
Confused	bewildered disoriented stunned baffled	puzzled doubtful helpless perplexed	unsure undecided uncertain lost
Strong	powerful potent forceful fearless	confident tough brave daring	capable adequate firm assured
Weak	ashamed exhausted powerless frail	vulnerable inept inadequate worn	unable tired shaken weary

Recommended Readings

Ackerman, D. (1990). *A natural history of the sense*. New York, NY: Random House.

Alicke, M., Dunning, D., & Krueger, J. (2005) *The self in social judgment*, New York, NY: Psychology Press.

Andre, R. (1995). Leading diverse management teams in logistics. *Journal of Business Logistics*. 16(2), 65, 20.

Aspy, D., & Roebuck, E. (1984). *Kids don't learn from people they don't like* (2nd ed.). Amherst, MA: Human Resources Development Press.

Baytos, L. M. (Oct: 1995). Task forces drive successful diversity efforts. *HR Magazine, 40*(10), 95, 4.

Buhler, P. (March 1997). Managing in the 90s. *Supervision, 58*(3).

Cacioppo, J. T., & Patrick, W. (2008). *Loneliness, "human nature," and the need for social connection*. New York, NY: WW Norton & Co.

Carkhuff, R. R. (2008). *Art of helping IX*. Amherst, MA: Human Resource Development Press.

Doka, K. J. (May/June 1996). Dealing with diversity: the coming challenge to American business. *Business Horizons, 39*(3), 67, 5.

Ekman, P., & Friesen, W. V. (2003). *Unmasking the face*. Malor Books.

Ferguson, J. T.; Johnson, W. R. (Sept. 1995). Managing diversity. *Mortgage Banking, 55*(12), 33, 4.

Fisher, H. (2004). *The nature and chemistry of romantic love*. New York, NY: Henry Holt & Co.

Gardner, H. (1993). *Multiple intelligence*. New York, NY: Basic Books.

Gladwell, M.(2002). The tipping point. New York, NY: Back Bay Books.

Gladwell, M. (2008). *Outliers*, New York, NY: Little, Brown, & Co.

Hames, D. S. (May 1996). Training in the land of Doone: an exercise in understanding cultural differences. *Journal of Management Education, 20*(2), 258, 7.

Knapp, M., & Daly, J. (1994). *Handbook of interpersonal communication* (2nd Ed.). Thousand Oaks, CA: Sage Publications.

Kowalski, R. (ed.) (2001). *Behaving badly.* Ashington, DC: American Psychological Association.

Lewis, J. (May/June 1996). Practicing diversity awareness. *Women in Business,* 48(3), 28, 4.

Mager, R. (1972). *Goal analysis.* Atlanta, GA: Center for Effective Performance.

Managing diversity. A Monthly Source of Information, Ideas and Tips for People Managing a Diverse Workforce. http://www.utexas.edu/tudent/housing/odd/oddresources/OrganizationalDiversityandDevelopment.htm

McDonald, T. (February 1996). Worldwide appeal. *Successful Meetings,* 45(2), 26, 1.

Minorities advance in management jobs. (Sept. 1995). *HR Focus, 72*(9), 20, 1/3.

Rice, F. & Faircloth, A. Denny's changes its spots. *Fortune, 133*(9), 133, 5.

Roberts, R. (April 1996). Fostering diversity. *Pittsburgh Business Times, 15*(37), Minority Business Times, 6, 2.

Sen. Sankar & Hill, R. P. (Fall 1996). Marketing and minority civil rights: the case of Amendment 2 and the Colorado boycott. *Journal of Public Policy & Marketing, 15*(2), 311, 8.

Sampson, S. J., Blakeman, J. D., & Carkhuff, R. R. (2006). Social intelligence skills for correctional officers. Amherst, MA: Human Resource Development Press.

Sampson, S. J., Blakeman, J. D., & Carkhuff, R. R. (2006). Social intelligence skills for correctional supervisors/managers. Amherst, MA: Human Resource Development Press.

Sampson, S. J., Blakeman, J. D., & Carkhuff, R. R. (2006). Social intelligence skills for government supervisors/managers. Amherst, MA: Human Resource Development Press.

Sampson, S. J., Blakeman, J. D., & Carkhuff, R. R. (2006). Social intelligence skills for law enforcement officers. Amherst, MA: Human Resource Development Press.

Sampson, S. J., Blakeman, J. D., & Carkhuff, R. R. (2006). Social intelligence skills for law enforcement supervisors/managers. Amherst, MA: Human Resource Development Press.

Sampson, S. J., Blakeman, J. D., & Carkhuff, R. R. (2006). Social intelligence skills for sheriff department supervisors/managers. Amherst, MA: Human Resource Development Press.

Sampson, S. J., & Elrod, C. (2007). *How to be in a personal relationship.* Amherst, MA: Human Resource Development Press.

Schacter, D. (2001). *The seven sins of memory,* New York, NY: Houghton Mifflin.

Schor, S. M., Sims, R. R., et al. (May 1996). Power and diversity: sensitizing yourself and others through self-reflection and storytelling. *Journal of Management Education, 20*(2), 242, 16.

Solomon, C. M. (Oct. 1995). Unlock the potential of older workers. *Personnel Journal, 74*(10), 56, 8.

Sternberg, R., & Weis, K. (2006). *The new psychology of love.* Binghampton, NY: Yale University.

Van Auken, P. (1996). International business realities that affect supervisors. *Supervision,* (57), 8.

References

Ahmed, S. M. S. (1979). Visibility of the victim. *The Journal of Social Psychology, 107,* 253–255.

Aloni, M., & Bernieri, F. J. (2004). Is love blind? The effects of experience and infatuation on the perception of love. *Journal of Nonverbal Behavior, 28,* 287–296.

Anderson, L., & Pearson, C. (1999). Tit for tat? The spiraling effect of incivility in the workplace. *The Academy of Management Review, 24,* 452-471.

Arnold, K. D. (1995). Lives of Promise: What Becomes of High School Valedictorians. San Francisco, CA: Jossey-Bass.

Aspy, C. Brown, H., Hancock, M., Jonas, A., & Aspy, D. (1998). The effects of empathy on the amount of information in the medical history interview. Unpublished paper as cited in Aspy D., et al., 2000.

Aspy, C., & Sandhu, D. (1999). Empowering women for equity: A counseling approach. Alexandria, VA: American Counseling Association.

Aspy, D. (1972). A day of humanization in Arlington, Texas. *Educational Leadership, 29,* 703–707.

Aspy, D., Aspy, C., Russel, G., & Wedel, M. (1998). Winning America's Values War. Edmund, OK: The Center for the Systematic Study of Values and Virtues.

Aspy, D., Aspy, C. B., Russell, G., & Wedel, M. (2000). Carkhuff's Human Technology: A verification and extension of Kelly's (1997) suggestion to integrate the humanistic and technical components of counseling. *Journal of Counseling & Development, 78,* 29–37.

Aspy, D., & Roebuck, E. (1996). From humane ideas to humane technology and back again many times. In R. Cassel (ed.), Carl Rogers: Student-centered learning (pp. 63–71). Chula Vista, CA: Project Innovation.

Aspy, D., Russell, G., & Wedel, M. (1998a). How to participate in the national values conversation. Edmond, OK: The Center for the Systematic Study of Values and Virtues.

Aspy, D., Russell, G., & Wedel, M. (1998b). The 3L way to teach virtues to your kids. Edmond, OK: The Center for the Systematic Study of Values and Virtues.

Aspy, D., Russell, G., & Wedel, M. (1998c). How to teach Christian values to your kids. Edmond, OK: The Center for the Systematic Study of Values and Virtues.

Aspy, D., Russel, G., & Wedel, M (unk). Support for Patterson's advocacy of a universal system of multicultural counseling. *Journal of Multicultural Counseling and Development* (as cited in Aspy et al., 2000).

Bargh, J. A., Chen, M., & Burrows, L. (1996). Automaticity of social behavior: direct effects of trait construct and stereotype activation. *Journal of Personality and Social Psychology, 71,* 230–244.

Bauerle, S.Y., Amirkhan, J. H., & Hupka, R. B. (2002). An attribution theory analysis of romantic jealousy. *Motivation & Emotion, 26,* 297–319.

Baumeister, R. F., Zhang, L., & Vohs, K. D. (2004). Gossip as cultural learning. *Review of General Psychology, 2,* 111–121.

Blage, K. A., & Milner, J. (2000). Emotion recognition ability in mothers at high and low risk for child physical abuse. *International Journal of Child Abuse and Neglect, 24,* 1289–1298.

Bloom, R. B. (1977). Therapeutic management of children's profanity. *Behavioral Disorders, 2,* 205–211.

Bostrom, R. N., Basehart, J. R., & Rossiter, C. M. (1973). The effects of three types of profane language in persuasive messages. *Journal of Communication, 23,* 461–475.

Bouchard, T. J., & McGuire, M. (2003). Genetic and environmental influences on human psychological differences. *Journal of Neurobiology, 54,* pp. 4–45.

Social Intelligence Skills

Breckinridge-Church, R., Kelly, S. D., & Lynch, K. (2000). Immediate memory for mismatched speech and representational gesture across development. *Journal of Nonverbal Behavior, 24,* 151–174.

Brigman, G. A. (1991). The effects of student readiness training on the listening comprehension, attending, and social skills of kindergarten students. *Dissertation Abstracts, Georgia State University, College of Education,* order number 9131857.

Byron, K. (2002). Predicting work place success from nonverbal communication skills. *Unpublished doctoral dissertation. Department of Psychology, Georgia State University, Atlanta, GA.*

Cameron, P. (1969). Frequency and kinds of words in various social settings to what the hells' going on? *Pacific Sociological Review, 12,* 101–104.

Carkhuff, Robert R. (1974). Cry twice! Human Resources Development Press: Amherst, MA.

Carkhuff, Robert R. (1983a). Interpersonal Skills and Human Productivity. Human Resources Development Press: Amherst, MA.

Carkhuff, Robert R. (1983b). Sources of Human Productivity. Human Resources Development Press: Amherst, MA.

Carkhuff, Robert R. (1993). *The Art of Helping VII.* Human Resource Development Press: Amherst, MA.

Carkhuff, Robert R. (2000). *The Art of Helping in the 21st Century.* Human Resource Development Press: Amherst, MA.

Chapman, A. (2006). Mehrabian's communication research: Professor Albert Mehrabian's communication model [Electronic version]. http:businessball.com/mehrabiancommunications.htm

Church, R. B., Kelly, S. D., & Lynch, K. (2000). Immediate memory for mismatched speech and representational gesture across development. *Journal of Nonverbal Behavior, 24*(2), 151–174.

Collingswood, T. Douds, A., Williams, H., & Wilson, R. D. (1978). Developing youth resources. Carkhuff Institute of Human Technology: Amherst, MA.

Davidson, R. J., Shackman, A. J., & Maxwell, J. S. (2004). Asymmetries in face and brain related to emotion. *Trends in Cognitive Science, 8,* 389–391.

Day, S., Matheny, K., & Megathlin, W. (1977). Training corre ctional personnel in the helping skills. *Alabama Personnel and Guidance Journal*, 15–24.

DeBacker, C. J. S., Nelissen, M., & Fisher, M. L. (2007). Let's talk about sex: a study on the recall of gossip about potential mates and sexual rivals. *Sex Roles, 56*, 781–791.

DiBaise, R., & Gunnoe, J. (2004). Gender and culture differences in touching behavior. *Journal of Social Psychology, 144*, 49–62.

Dijkstra, P., & Buunk, B. P. (2002). Sex differences in the jealousy-evoking effect of rival characteristics. *European Journal of Social Psychology, 32*, 829–852.

Dreyfuss, S.E., & Dreyfus, H. L. (1980). A Five-stage model of the mental activities involved in directed skill acquisition. The Operations Research Center. University of California, Berkeley. http://en.wikipedia.org/wiki/Dreyfus_model_of_skill_acquisition

Duncan, S. (1972). Some signals and rules for taking speaking turns in conversations. *Journal of Personality and Social Psychology, 23*, 283–292.

Duncan, S. (1969). Nonverbal communications. *Psychological Bulletin, 72*, 118–137.

Dunning, D. (2005). *Self-insight: roadblocks and detours on the path to knowing thyself*. New York, NY: Psychology Press: USA.

Elfenbein, H. A. (2006). Learning in emotion judgments: training and the cross-cultural understanding of facial expressions. *Journal of Nonverbal Behavior, 30*, 21–36.

Ekman, P., Davidson, R. J., & Friesen, W. V. (1990). The Duchenne smile: emotional expression and brains psychology: II. *Journal of Personality and Social Psychology, 58*, 342–353.

Ekman, Paul. (2003). *Emotions revealed*. New York, NY: Henry Holt & Company.

Eskritt, M., & Lee, K. (2003). Do actions speak louder than words? Preschool children's use of the verbal-nonverbal consistency principle during inconsistent communications. *Journal of Nonverbal Behavior, 27*, 25–41.

Eubank, M., Collins, D, & Smith, N. (2002). Anxiety and ambiguity: it's all open to interpretation. *Journal of Sport & Exercise Psychology, 24*, 239–254.

Feldman, R. S., Tomasian, J. C., & Coats, E. J. (1999). Nonverbal deception abilities and adolescents' social competence: Adolescents with higher social skills are better liars. *Journal of Nonverbal Behavior, 23*, 237–249.

Foisey, M. L., Philippot, P., Verbanck, P., Pelc, I., Van Der Straten, G., & Kornreich, C. (2005). Emotional facial expression decoding impairment in persons dependent on multiple substances: impact of a history of alcohol dependence. *Journal of Studies on Alcohol, 66*, 663–681.

Foster, E. K. (2004). Research on gossip: taxonomy, methods, and future directions. *Review of General Psychology, 2*, 78–99.

Gardner, H. (1999). *Intelligence reframed, multiple intelligences for the 21st century*. New York, NY: Basic Books.

Gerrity, D. A. (2000). Male university employees' experiences of sexual harassment-related behaviors. *Psychology of Men & Masculinity, 12*, 140–151.

Gladwell, M. (2005). *Blink*. Back Bay Books: New York, NY.

Goleman, Daniel. (2006). *Social intelligence*. New York, NY: Bantam Books.

Goleman, D. (1998). *Working with emotional intelligence*. New York, NY: Bantam Books.

Goleman, D. (1995). *Emotional intelligence: why it can matter more than IQ*. New York, NY: Bantam Books.

Gorawara-Bhat, R., Cook, M. A., & Sachs, G. A. (2007). Nonverbal communication in doctor-elderly patient transactions (NDEPT): Development of a tool. *Patient Education and Counseling, 66*, 223–224.

Gould, S. J. (1981). *The Mismeasure of Man*. (NY: W. W. Norton, pp. 151-152) as cited in Osgood, R. L. (1984). *Intelligence testing and the field of learning disabilities: A historical and critical perspective. Learning Disability Quarterly, 7*, 343–348.

Guerin, B., & Miyazaki, Y. (2006). Analyzing rumors, gossip, and urban legends through their conversational properties. *The Psychological Record, 56,* 23–34.

Hall, J. A., Carter, J. D., & Horgan, T. G. (2001). Status role of nonverbal cues. *Journal of Nonverbal Behavior, 25,* 79–100.

Harris, C. R. (2003). A review of sex differences in sexual jealousy, including self-report data, psychophysiological responses, interpersonal violence, and morbid jealousy. *Personality & Social Psychology Review, 7,* 102–128.

Hebl, M. R., King, E. B., Glick, P., Singletary, S. L., & Kazama, S. (2007). Hostile and benevolent reactions toward pregnant women: complementary interpersonal punishments and rewards that maintain traditional roles. *Journal of Applied Psychology, 92,* 1499–1511.

Heilveil, I., & Muehleman, J. T. (1981). Nonverbal clues to deception in a psychotherapy analogue. *Psychotherapy: Theory, Research, & Practice, 18,* 329–335.

Heisel, M. J., & Mongrain, M. (2004). Facial expressions and ambivalence: Looking for conflict in all the right faces. *Journal of Nonverbal Behavior, 28,* 35–52.

Hertenstein, M. J. (2002). Touch: its communicative functions in infancy. *Human Development, 45,* 70–94.

Hertenstein, M. J., VerKamp, J. M., Kerestes, A. M., & Holmes, R. M. (2006). The communicative functions of touch in humans, nonhuman primates, and rats: a review and synthesis of the empirical research. *Genetic, Social, and General Psychology Monographs, 132,* 5–94.

Herz, R. (2007). *The Scent of Desire.* William Morrow: New York, NY.

Hess, U., Adams, R. B., & Kleck, R. E. (2004). Facial appearance, gender, and emotion expression. *Emotion, 4,* 378–388.

Heubusch, N. J. (1977). Some effects of counselor profanity in counseling. *Journal of Counseling Psychology, 24,* 456–458.

Hill, V., & Pillow, B. H. (2006). Children's understanding of reputations. *Journal of Genetic Psychology, 167,* 137–157.

Hodgins, H. S., & Belch, C. (2000). Interpersonal violence and nonverbal abilities. *Journal of Nonverbal Behavior, 24,* 3–24.

Hogh-Olesen, H. (2008). Human spatial behavior: the spacing of people, objects, and animals in six cross-cultural samples. *Journal of Cognition & Culture, 8,* 245–280.

Horstmann, G. (2003). What do facial expressions convey: feeling states, behavioral intentions, or action requests? *Emotion, 3,* 150–166.

Houmanfar, R., & Johnson, R. (2003). Organizational implications of gossip and rumor. *Journal of Organizational Behavior Management, we*(2–3), 117–138.

Indersmitten, T., & Gur, R. C. (2003). Emotion processing in chimeric faces: hemispheric asymmetries in expression and recognition of emotions. *The Journal of Neuroscience,* 3820–3825.

Jackson, M. (2008). *Distracted: the erosion of attention and the coming dark age.* New York, NY: Prometheus Books.

Johnson, P. R., & Indvik, J. (2001). Rudeness at work: Impulse over restraint. *Public Personnel Management, 30,* 457–465.

Kaye, B. K., & Sapolsky, B. S. (2004). Watch your mouth! An analysis of profanity uttered by children on prime-time television. *Mass Communication & Society, 7,* 429–452.

Keltner, D., & Shiota, M. N. (2003). New displays and new emotions: a commentary on Rozin and Cohen (2003). *Emotion, 3,* 86-91.

Kibby, M. D. (2005). E-mail forwardables: folklore in the age of the Internet. *New Media & Society, 7,* 770–790.

Kneidinger, L. M., Maple, T. L., & Tross, S. A. (2001). Touching behavior in sport: functional components, analysis of sex differences, and ethological considerations. *Journal of Nonverbal Behavior, 25,* 43–62.

Kohler, C. G., Turner, T., Stolar, N. M., Bilker, W. B., Brensinger, C. M., Gur, R. E., & Gur, R. C. (2004). Differences in facial expressions of four universal emotions. *Psychiatry Research, 128,* 235–244.

Kornreich, C., Philippot, P., Foisy, M. L., Blairy, S., Raynaud, E., Dan, B., Hess, U., Noel, X., Pelc, I., & Verbanck, P. (2002). Impaired emotional facial expression recognition is associated with interpersonal problems in alcoholism. *Alcohol & Alcoholism, 37,* 394–400.

Krumm, D. (2001). *Psychology at work: an introduction to industrial organizational psychology.* New York: Worth Publishers.

Kurklen, R., & Kassinove, H. (1991). Effects of profanity, touch, and subject's religiosity on perceptions of a psychologist and behavioral compliance. *The Journal of Social Psychology, 131,* 899–901.

LaFrance, M. (1992). Gender and interruptions: individual infraction of violation of the social order? *Psychology of Women Quarterly, 16,* 497–512.

LaPlante, D., & Ambady, N. (2000). Multiple messages: facial recognition advantage for compound expressions. *Journal of Nonverbal Behavior, 24,* 211–224.

LaPointe, L. L. (2006). Profanity. *Journal of Medical Speech-Language Pathology, 14,* vii–ix.

Larkin, K. T., Martin, R. R., & McClain, S. E. (2002). Cynical hostility and the accuracy of decoding facial expressions of emotions. *Journal of Behavioral Medicine, 25,* 285–292.

Lee, V., & Wagner, H. (2002). The effect of social presence on the facial and verbal expression of emotion and the interrelationships among emotional components. *Journal of Nonverbal Behavior, 26,* 3–25.

Leppanen, J. M., Milders, M., Bell, J. S., Terriere, E., & Hietanen, J. K. (2004). Depression biases the recognition of emotionally neutral faces. *Psychiatry Research, 128,* 123–133.

Ludwig, T., & Barkhurst, M. (2003). Intervention Skills Training for managing the Mentally Ill Inmate. Presentation to the Broward Sheriff's Office, October.

Marelich, W. D. (2002). Effects of behavior settings, extradyadic behaviors, and interloper characteristics on romantic jealousy. *Social Behavior & Personality: An International Journal, 30,* 785–794.

Marrazziti, D., Rucci, P., Di Nasso, E., Masala, I., Baroni, S., Rossi, A., Giannaccini, G., Mengali, F., & Lucacchini, A. (2003). Jealousy and subthreshold psychopathology: A serotonergic link. *Neuropsychobiology, 47,* 6–12.

Mast, M. S., & Hall, J. A. (2004). Who is the boss and who is not? Accuracy judging and status. *Journal of Nonverbal Behavior, 28,* 145–165.

McAndrew, F. T., Bell, E. K., & Garcia, C. M. (2007). Who do we tell and whom do we tell on? Gossip as a strategy for status enhancement. *Journal of Applied Social Psychology, 37,* 1562–1577.

McDonald, S. (2000). Neuropsychological studies of sarcasm. *Metaphor and Symbol, 15,* 85–98.

McPherson, W. (2008). Managing the Mental Health Population at the Broward Sheriff's Office. *Corrections Today, June.*

Melfsen, S., & Florin, I. (2002). Do socially anxious children show deficits in classifying facial expressions of emotions? *Journal of Nonverbal Behavior, 26,* 109–126.

Mesoudi, A., Whiten, A., & Dunbar, R. (2006). A bias for social information in human cultural transmission. *British Journal of Psychology, 97,* 405–423.

Mignault, A., & Chaudhuri, A. (2003). The many faces of a neutral face: Head tilt and perception of dominance and emotion. *Journal of Nonverbal Behavior, 27,* 111–132.

Milgram, S. (1965). Some conditions of obedience and disobedience to authority. *Human Relationships, 18,* 57–75.

Mitchell, J. (2001). Identification of emotional cues in facial cues and tones of voice in adolescents with a history of sexual offenses. Unpublished manuscript, Department of Psychology, Emory University, Atlanta, GA.

Montepare, J. M., & Dobish, H. (2003). The contribution of emotion perceptions and their overgeneralizations to trait impressions. *Journal of Nonverbal Behavior, 27,* 237–254.

Moszkowski, R. J., & Stack, D. M. (2007). Infant touching behavior during mother-infant face-to-face interactions. *Infant & Child Development, 16,* 307–319.

Mullins, D. T., & Duke, M. P. (2004). Effects of social anxiety on nonverbal accuracy ad response time: facial expressions. *Journal of Nonverbal Behavior, 28,* 3–33.

Nerbonne, G. P., & Hipskind, N. M. (1972). The use of profanity in conversational speech. *Journal of Communications Disorders, 5,* 47–50.

Okada, T., Murai, T., Kubota, Y., & Sato, W. (2003). Impaired recognition of emotional facial expressions in schizophrenia across cultures. *Clinical Psychiatry, 45,* 535–541.

Paradise, L. V., Cohl, B., & Zweig, J. (1980). Effects of profane language and physical attractiveness on perceptions of counselor behavior. *Journal of Counseling Psychology, 27,* 620–624.

Parkes, C. M., & Benjamin, B., & Fitzgerald, R. G. (1969). Broken Heart: A Statistical Study of Increased Mortality among Widowers. *British Medical Journal, (5646),* 740–743.

Patterson, C. H. (1996). Multicultural counseling: from diversity to universality. *Journal of Counseling & Development, 74,* 227–231.

Pendleton, S. C. (1998). Rumor research revisited and expanded. *Language and Communication, 18,* 69–86.

Phillips, K. A., Didie, E. R., Feusner, J., & Wilhelm, S. (2008). Body dysmorphic disorder: Treating an unrecognized disorder. *The American Journal of Psychiatry, 165,* 1111–1120.

Pitterman, H., & Nowicki, S. (2004). The test of the ability to identify emotion in human standing and sitting postures: the diagnostic analysis of nonverbal accuracy-2 posture test (DANVA2-POS). *Genetic, Social, and General Psychology Monographs, 130*(2), 146–162.

Porath, C. L., & Erez, A. (2007). Does rudeness really matter? The effects of rudeness on task performance and helpfulness. *Academy of Management Journal, 50,* 1181–1197.

Puente, S., & Cohen, D. (2003). Jealousy and the meaning (or nonmeaning) of violence. *Personality & Social Psychology Bulletin, 29,* 449–460.

Putnam, R. (2000). *Bowling alone.* New York, NY: Simon & Schuster.

Social Intelligence Skills

Ray, G. B., & Floyd, K. (2006). Nonverbal expressions of liking and disliking in initial interaction: encoding and decoding perspectives. *Southern Communication Journal, 71,* 45–65.

Regan, P. C., Darell, J., Narvaez, M., & Johnson, D. (1999). Public displays of affection among Asian and Latino heterosexual couples. *Psychological Reports, 84,* 1201–1202.

Ribi, R. F., Yokoyama, A., & Turner, D. C. (2008). Comparison of children's behavior toward Sony's robotic dog AIBO and a real dog: A pilot study. *Anthrozoos, 21,* 245–256.

Ripley, K. N. (1998). The effects of interpersonal management skills training on the families of persons with mental illness. *Dissertation Abstracts International: Section B: The Sciences and Engineering, 59(2-B).*

Rocha, L. (1985). Educational productivity in Brazil. In D. Aspy, & E. Roebuck (Eds.), The third century in American education (pp. 99–102). Amherst, MA: Human Resources Development Press.

Rosnow, R. L. (2001). Rumor and gossip in interpersonal interaction and beyond: a social exchange perspective. In R. M. Kowalski (Ed.), *Behaving badly: Aversive behaviors in interpersonal relationships* (pp. 203–232). Washington, DC: American Psychological Association.

Rothman, A. D., & Nowicki, S. (2004). A measure of the ability to identify emotion in children's tone of voice. *Journal of Nonverbal Behavior, 28,* 67–92.

Salovey, P. & Mayer, J. (1990). Emotional Intelligence. *Imagination, Cognition, and Personality (9),* 185–211.

Sato, W., Kubota, Y., Okada, T., Murai, T., Yoshikawa, S., & Sengoku, A. (2002). Seeing happy emotion in fearful and angry faces: Qualitative analysis of facial expression recognition in a bilateral amygdala-damaged patient. *Cortex, (38),* 727–742.

Savage, J. E., & Tapley, R. (1976). The dozens. *Transactional Analysis Journal, 6,* 18–20.

Sazar, L., & Kassinove, H. (1991). Effects of counselor's profanity and subject's religiosity on content acquisition of a counseling lecture and behavioral compliance. *Psychological Reports, 69,* 1059–1070.

Selnow, G. W. (1985). Sex differences in uses and perceptions of profanity. *Sex Roles, 12,* 303–312.

Sencius, A. H., Wesolowski, M. D., & Burke, W. H. (1990). The use of visual cue to reduce profanity in a brain injured adult. *Behavioral Residential Treatment, 5,* 143–147.

Sewell, E. H. (1984). Appreciation of cartoons with profanity captions. *Psychological Reports, 54,* 583–587.

Shamay-Tsoory, S. G., Tomer, T. & Aharon-Peretz, J. (2007). The neuroanatomical basis of understanding sarcasm and its relationship to social cognition. *Neuropsychology, 19,* 288–300.

Smith, E. E., & White, H. L. (1965). Wit, creativity, and sarcasm. *Journal of Applied Psychology 49,* 131–134.

Smoot, S. L., & Gonzalez, J. L. (1995). Cost-effective communication skills training for state hospital employees. *Psychiatric Services, 46,* 819–823.

Sprouse, C. A., Hall, C. W., Webster, R. E., & Bolen, L. M. (1998). Social perception in students with learning disabilities and attention-deficit/hyperactivity disorder. *Journal of Nonverbal Behavior, 22,* 125–134.

Sternberg, R. (1997). *Successful Intelligence.* New York, NY: The Penguin Group.

Sternglanz, R. W., & DePaulo, B. M. (2004). Reading nonverbal cues to emotions: The advantages and liabilities of relationship closeness. *Journal of Nonverbal Behavior, 28,* 245–266.

Sullivan, S., & Ruffman, T. (2004). Emotion recognition deficits in the elderly. *International Journal of Neuroscience, 114,* 403–432.

Svoboda, E. (July–August 2007). Sarcastic masters: they're smart, they're funny, and they know it. But is cracking jokes that put other people down truly wise? *Psychology Today,* 43–44.

Teranova, S. (2002). Predicting success of salespeople. Unpublished master's thesis, Department of Psychology, Emory University, Atlanta, GA.

Terneus, S. K., & Malone, Y. (2004). Proxemics and kinesics of adolescents in dual-gender groups. *Guidance & Counseling, 19,* 118–123.

Thompson, L. A., Aidinejad, M. R., & Ponte, J. (2001). Aging and the effects of facial and prosodic cues on emotional intensity ratings and memory constructions. *Journal of Nonverbal Behavior, 2002,* 101–125.

Townshend, J. M., & Duka, T. (2003). Mixed emotions: alcoholics' impairments in the recognition of specific emotional facial expressions. *Neuropsychologia, 41,* 773–782.

Turman, P. D. (2003). Coaches and cohesion: The impact of coaching techniques on team cohesion in the small group sport setting. *Journal of sport Behavior, 26,* 86–105.

Vaillant, George. (1977). Adaptation to life. Boston, MA: Little & Brown.

Vaillant, George, & Davis, J. Timothy. (2000). Social/Emotional intelligence and midlife resilience in school boys with low tested intelligence. *American Journal of Orthopsychiatry, 70*(2), 215–222.

Vettine, J., & Todt, D. (2004). Laughter in conversation: features of occurrence and acoustic structure. *Journal of Nonverbal Behavior, 28,* 93–115.

Von Knorring, A., Soderberg, A., Austin, L., & Uvnas-Moberg, K. (2008). Massage decreases aggression in preschool children: a long-term study. *Acta Paediatrica, 97,* 1265–1269.

Vorauer, J. D., Cameron, J. J., Holmes, J. G., & Pearce, D. G. (2003). Invisible overtures: Fears of rejection and the signal amplification bias. *Journal of Personality & Social Psychology, 85,* 793–812.

Wagner, R. K. (2002). *Smart people doing dumb things,* in *Why smart people can be so stupid.* Robert Sternberg (Ed). New Haven, CT: Yale University.

Weiskrantz, L. (1995). Blindsight—not an island unto itself. *Current Directions in Psychological Science, 4,* 146–151.

Wert, S. R., & Salovey, P. (2004). A social comparison account of gossip. *Review of General Psychology, 8,* 122–137.

White, S. (2000). Conceptual foundations of IQ testing. *Psychology, Public Policy, and Law, 6*(1), 33–43.

Winner, E., Windmueller, G., Rosenblatt, E., Bosco, L., Best, E., & Gardner, H. (1987). Making sense of literal and nonliteral falsehood. *Metaphor and Symbolic Activity, 2*, 13–32.

Zangara, A., Blair, R. J. R., & Curran, H. V. (2002). A comparison of the effects of β-adrenergic blocker and a benzodiazepine upon the recognition of human facial expressions. *Psychopharmacology, 2002*, 36–41.

Zencius, A. H., Weslowski, M. D., Burke, W. H. (1990). The use of visual cue to reduce profanity in a brain injured adult. *Behavioral Residential Treatment, 5*(3), 143–147.

About the Authors

Stephen J. Sampson, Ph.D.

Dr. Steve Sampson is the founder and president of SoTelligence, Inc. As an entrepreneur and academician, he brings both academic knowledge and practical experience to your training experience.

As an educator, he holds a bachelors degree in Sociology from the University of Massachusetts (1970) and a master's (1976) and a doctoral degree (1981) in Counseling Psychology from Georgia State University. He is a nationally recognized master trainer in interpersonal communication skills since 1977 and has presented that training to over 300 agencies and organizations in 40 states. He is a former assistant professor of Criminal Justice at Georgia State University from 1979 to 1985. More recently, he retired from his position as a clinical professor in the Counseling and Psychological Services Department at Georgia State University (1995 to 2004).

As a licensed psychologist, he is the former chief of psychology of Georgia Regional Hospital, Atlanta, Georgia (1993 to 1995). He is also a nationally recognized counseling psychologist who works with various law enforcement agencies conducting fitness for duty evaluations and post shooting debriefings since 1982. He has been a contract psychologist with 25 metropolitan Atlanta law enforcement agencies since 1991.

As a criminologist, Dr. Sampson is the former correctional superintendent for Massachusetts Halfway Houses Inc. (1969 to 1973), as well as the former correctional superintendent for the Georgia Department of Corrections (1974 to 1976). He has provided training to over 250 prisons, law enforcement, and public safety agencies in social skills training since 1977.

As an author, he has published the following books on social intelligence skills:

- *Social Intelligence Skills for Law Enforcement Supervisors/ Managers*
- *Social Intelligence Skills for Law Enforcement Officers*
- *Social Intelligence Skills for Correctional Supervisors/Managers*
- *Social Intelligence Skills for Correctional Officers*
- *Social Intelligence Skills for Government Managers*
- *Social Intelligence Skills for Sheriff's Department Supervisors/ Managers*

His most recent book is *How to Be in a Personal Relationship* (HRD Press, Inc., www.hrd.com).

Cindy Elrod, Ph.D.

Cindy Elrod, a community/organizational psychologist (Georgia State University [GSU]), provides consultation to a variety of public, private, and government agencies, providing job analyses, leadership, and customer service training; program evaluations; 360° analysis and feedback; and leadership coaching.

As a consultant to SoTelligence, Inc., Cindy works with Dr. Steve Sampson, developing and presenting training in the areas of social and emotional intelligence, stress and time management, verbal and non-verbal communication, conflict management, and diversity. She is a co-author of *How to Be in a Personal Relationship.*

In 2005, Cindy completed a term appointment with the Veterans Administration at the National Center for Post-Traumatic Stress Disorder (NCPTSD; White River Junction, Vermont). As project manager and qualitative analysis expert, she and the team evaluated the Federal Emergency Management Agency's (FEMA) process for implementing a disaster mental health response program in communities with declarations of natural, technological, or intentional disasters (see *The Annals of the American Academy of Political and Social Science,* March, 2006).

Cindy was an award-winning visiting lecturer and instructor with GSU's Department of Psychology (1999 to 2003), teaching a variety of classes, including group process and dynamics, behavior modification, learning, abnormal psychology, and environmental and social influences on behavior. Her research has focused on human response to transitions, psychological contracts, job satisfaction, followership, organizational character, social participation, perceived social support, and sense of community. As a social scientist, she has won numerous awards for her research and has been recognized for contributions in the areas of relationships, organizational influences on behavior, and institutionalized aging.

Cindy came to the teaching and consulting fields after 22 years with Delta Air Lines, working her way up from agent to management in Field Services (ramp operations, fueling, baggage service, gates/ticketing). Some of her accomplishments included designing and implementing a departmental reorganization and authoring and implementing training in conflict negotiation, airline emergency preparedness and response, and frontline leadership basics.